PRIMARY PARTNERS

A- Z Activities
to Make Learning Fun

for Ages 4-7
(CHOOSE THE RIGHT B)

Fun-to-Make Visuals ◘ Copy-and-Create Crafts

Simple Supplies Needed ◘ Matching Thought Treats

USE FOR PRIMARY LESSONS AND FAMILY HOME EVENING

to Reinforce Gospel Topics

You'll Find: A-Z Topics to Match Primary Lessons

Accountability   Atonement   Baptismal Covenants   Baptism

Book of Mormon   Choose the Right   Christmas   Commandments

Do Unto Others   Easter   Example   Faith   Fasting   First Vision

Forgive   Heavenly Father's Plan   Holy Ghost   Honoring

Joseph Smith's Childhood   Love   Missionaries   Obedience

Parents   Pray   Prayer   Priesthood   Prophets

Pure and Righteous   Repentance   Restoration   Sacrament   Service

Temples and Families   Tithing   Word of Wisdom   Worshipping at Church

97 98 99 00 01   10 9 8 7 6 5 4 3 2

Primary Partners: Ages 4–7, Choose The Right-B

Covenant Communications, Inc.
ISBN 1-57734-034-5

INTRODUCTION
PRIMARY PARTNERS
A-Z Activities to Make Learning Fun
for Choose the Right B   Ages 4-7

Children and parents alike will love the easy, fun-to-create visuals contained in this volume. Patterns for each of the projects are actual size, ready to Copy-n-Create in minutes. You'll enjoy using many of the Primary Partners crafts and activities to supplement the Primary 3* lessons, enhance your family home evenings, and help children learn gospel principles in fun, creative ways.

HOW TO USE THIS BOOK

1. **Preview A-Z Table of Contents** to find pictures and subjects.
2. **Use Lesson Cross Reference Index** on page iv. Match your lesson number with the A-Z subject to find activities quickly.
3. **Shop Ahead for Simple Supplies.** Each activity requires a few basic items: Copies of patterns, scissors, tape, glue, crayons, zip-close plastic bags, boxes, paper punch, yarn or ribbon, string, wooden craft sticks, metal brads, removable tape, page reinforcements, small bandages, 8-ounce styrofoam cups, potting soil, and sticks of gum.
4. **Copy Patterns Ahead.** You'll save time and avoid last-minute preparation.
5. **Organize Activities** in an A-Z file. Copy instructions to include with the pattern copies and supplies.
6. **Reward for Reverence.** Copy a reverence chart and set of bear glue-on stickers (page ii and iii) for each child. When children are reverent during the lesson reward them with a bear they can glue on their chart (weeks #1-47). If they are not as reverent as they should be, don't give them a bear (or cut a bear in half). The next week when they see their chart, they are reminded of what they need to do to earn a bear-y fun reward. Tell children that Jesus wants us to be bear-y reverent in Heavenly Father's house.

I have been BEARY reverent!

☺	☺	☺	☺	5	6	7	8	9
10	11	12	13	14	15	16	17	18
19	20	21	22	23	24	25	26	27
28	29	30	31	32	33	34	35	36
37	38	39	40	41	42	43	44	45
46	47							

Clayton K. -NAME-

7. **Activity Storage Box.** Create a CTR fun box to store classroom creations and encourage children to bear their testimony of gospel principles.

You'll Need: Copy of I CAN BEAR MY TESTIMONY CTR FUN BOX label (bear's tummy), bear's arms and legs, and Dear Parents note (page 84), and a shoe or shirt box for each child, scissors, glue, contact paper, and crayons.

TO MAKE BOX:

Step #1: Cover box with contact paper.

Step #2: Color and cut out label and glue-on stickers.

Step #3: Glue label and stickers on box.

Step #4: Send home the Dear Parents note (glue on inside lid or tape on top).

*Primary 3-CTR B manual is published by The Church of Jesus Christ of Latter-day Saints, Salt Lake City, Utah.

i

I have been BEARY reverent!

1	2	3	4	5	6	7	8	9
10	11	12	13	14	15	16	17	18
19	20	21	22	23	24	25	26	27
28	29	30	31	32	33	34	35	36
37	38	39	40	41	42	43	44	45
46	47							

NAME:

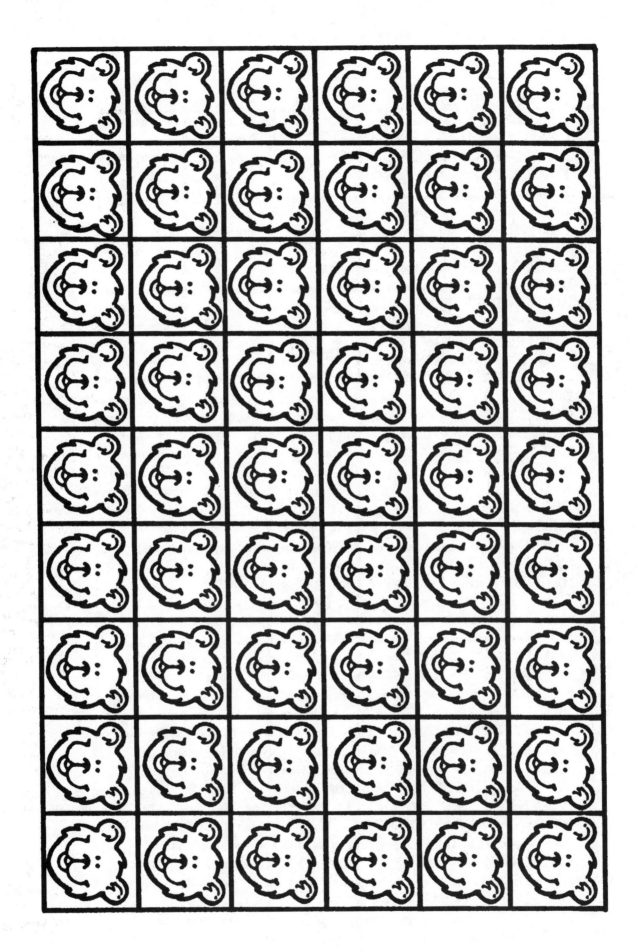

*Primary 3-CTR B manual is published by The Church of Jesus Christ of Latter-day Saints, Salt Lake City, Utah.

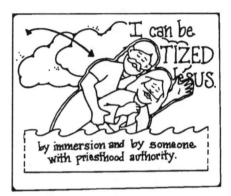

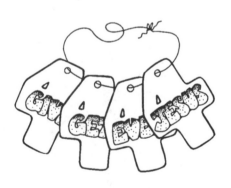

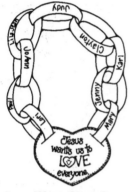

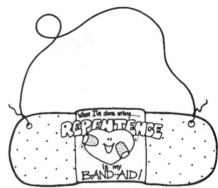

A

ACCOUNTABILITY: Eight Is Great! -- Age of Accountability

(Annabell Accountable ... the "udderly" responsible cow)

See lesson #27 in Primary 3-CTR B manual*.

YOU'LL NEED: Copy of cow and cow spots patterns (page 2) on white cardstock paper for each child, scissors, glue, and crayons

ACTIVITY: Remind child that at age eight they can be baptized. Say, "Let's learn how to make right choices before baptism. We can be accountable, or responsible for our actions. Let's create Annabell the accountable cow who is utterly responsible for her actions. Each spot shows ways you can be accountable."
1. Color and cut out cow picture and spots (flaps) to cover accountable actions.
2. Fold the matching cow spot flaps.
3. Glue flaps on cow's matching spots (spot can flip open to read the accountable action, i.e. "clean room").

THOUGHT TREAT: Give children 8 Milk Duds® candy, a sugar cookie in the shape of an 8, or 8 cow caramel or taffy candies. Children can share 8 ways they can be "udderly" responsible like Annabell Accountable cow as they moo-ve toward baptism.

ATONEMENT: I Can Repent and Be Forgiven ... Because of Jesus

(repentance wheel)

See lesson #22 in Primary 3-CTR B manual*.

YOU'LL NEED: Copy of repentance wheel pattern (pages 3-4) on colored cardstock paper, a metal or button brad for each child, scissors, and crayons

ACTIVITY: Because Jesus Christ atoned for our sins, we can repent. Make and turn the repentance wheel to see if each child can "Wheelie Repent."
1. Color and cut out repentance wheels.
2. Attach part A on top of part B with a metal or button brad.

To Make Button Brad: Sew two buttons together on opposite sides (threading thread through the same hole) to attach repentance wheels.

THOUGHT TREAT: <u>Smile and Frown Sugar Cookies</u>. Eat frown cookie thinking of something they can repent of. Eat smile cooking thinking that they have repented and are choosing the right.

PATTERN: ATONEMENT (repentance wheel - part B)   See lesson #22 in Primary 3-CTR B manual*.

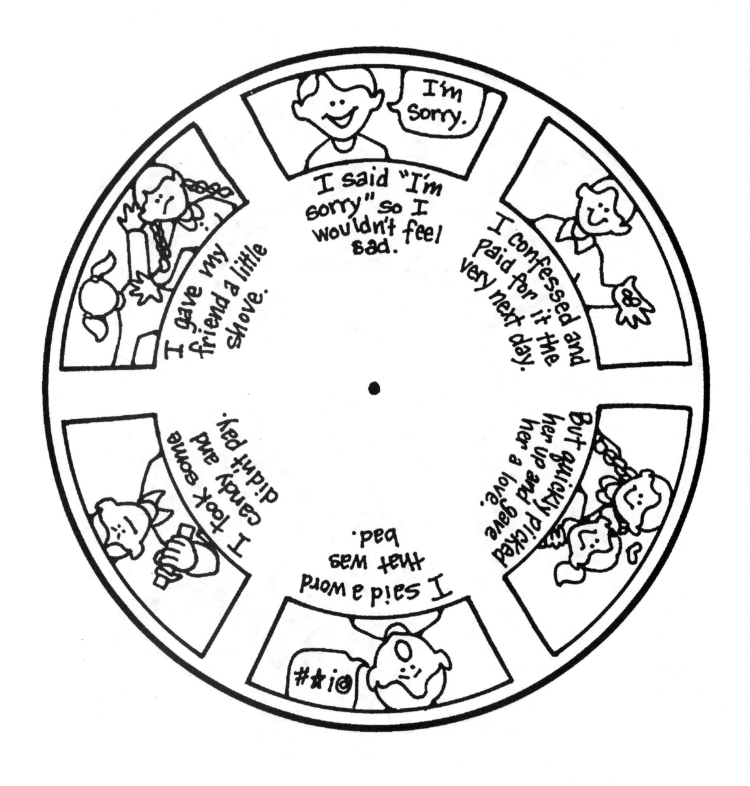

4   *Primary 3-CTR B manual is published by The Church of Jesus Christ of Latter-day Saints, Salt Lake City, Utah.

B

BAPTISMAL COVENANTS: I Promise and Heavenly Father Promises

(two-sided puzzle)

See lesson #13 in Primary 3-CTR B manual*.

YOU'LL NEED: Copy of two-sided puzzle pattern (page 6) on colored cardstock paper, an envelope or zip-close plastic sandwich bag to store puzzle pieces for each child, glue, and scissors, and crayons

ACTIVITY: Create a two-sided puzzle with child's baptism promises on one side and Heavenly Father's promises on the other side.
1. Color pictures.
2. Fold on dividing line back-to-back.
3. Glue sides together (spreading glue over the entire piece, not just the edges).
4. Trim edges. Cut puzzle shapes out as shown on one side (into six pieces).
5. Place puzzle pieces in an individual envelope or zip-close plastic sandwich bag. Give one to each child to find the puzzle message.

THOUGHT TREAT: Promise Handprint Cookie. Show child that we often raise our hand to promise things. You can count the child's promises on five fingers and Heavenly Father's promises on the other five fingers (the promises written on the puzzle). To make cookies, roll sugar or peanut butter cookie dough into a ball and flatten. Press a small child's handprint in dough. Bake 350° for 8-10 minutes. Before baking, sprinkle colored sugar in handprint impression. To color sugar, mix sugar and food coloring by shaking mixture in a bottle. Or, instead of colored sugar, paint handprint impression with cookie paint (mix two teaspoons canned milk with food coloring).

BAPTISM: Blessings from Baptism into Jesus Christ's Church

(picture word poster with glue-on stickers)

See lesson #21 in Primary 3-CTR B manual*.

YOU'LL NEED: Copy of poster and glue-on sticker patterns (page 7) on colored cardstock paper for each child, scissors, glue, and crayons

ACTIVITY: Create a poster to remind children of the blessings that come from being a member of The Church of Jesus Christ of Latter-day Saints. Blessings begin with baptism.
1. Color and cut out baptism poster and glue-on stickers.
2. Read the poster together and glue on stickers.

THOUGHT TREAT: Baptism Blessing Biscuits. Wrap wordstrip patterns in foil and place in the center of biscuit dough or muffin batter before baking--one message for each child. As children eat, have them find the message. Read message aloud. Messages match words on poster.

I PROMISE...

- To obey the commandments
- To read the scriptures
- To honor parents, help others
- To pay tithing
- To attend Primary + Sacrament meeting

Heavenly Father PROMISES...

- To forgive me when I repent.
- To love and bless me.
- To give me the gift of the Holy Ghost
- To answer my prayers
- To let me live with him forever

*Primary 3-CTR B manual is published by The Church of Jesus Christ of Latter-day Saints, Salt Lake City, Utah.

BAPTISIMAL PROMISES

When I am baptized:

- ☐ ☐ come a new member of the ☐.
- ☐ will receive the ☐ of the Holy ☐.
- ☐ ☐ be ☐ given by ☐ ly Father.

B

BAPTISM: I Can Be Baptized Like Jesus

(baptism by immersion 3-D pull-up card)

See lesson #11 in Primary 3-CTR B manual*.

YOU'LL NEED:
Copy of baptism font and figure patterns (page 9) on cardstock paper, and a metal or button brad for each child, scissors, glue, and crayons

ACTIVITY:
Create a baptism scene to show how children can be baptized by immersion like Jesus. A brad allows the figure to move in and out of the three dimensional water below.
1. Color and cut out water, figures, and scene.
2. Attach baptism figures with a metal or button brad where indicated.

To Make a Button Brad: Sew two buttons together on opposite sides (threading thread through the same hole) to attach figure to paper.

3. Fan-fold water tabs and glue to scene.
4. Move figures down to immerse in water.

THOUGHT TREAT:
Birthday Cake with Eight (8) Candles.
Don't light candles in meeting house, but pretend to blow them out. Each candle can represent ways to get ready for baptism:

- Candle #1 Pray daily.
- Candle #2 Attend Primary and sacrament meeting each week.
- Candle #3 Learn about the scriptures.
- Candle #4 Be honest.
- Candle #5 Pay tithing.
- Candle #6 Be kind to family and friends.
- Candle #7 Follow in the steps of Jesus.
- Candle #8 Be eight years old and be interviewed by the bishop or branch president.

Place candles on the cake as you name #1-8.

*Primary 3-CTR B manual is published by The Church of Jesus Christ of Latter-day Saints, Salt Lake City, Utah.

I can be BAPTIZED like Jesus.

by immersion and by someone, with Priesthood authority.

*Primary 3-CTR B manual is published by The Church of Jesus Christ of Latter-day Saints, Salt Lake City, Utah.

9

B

BOOK OF MORMON: The Golden Plates

(Hill Cumorah two-sided pop-up card)

See lesson #15 in Primary 3-CTR B manual*.

YOU'LL NEED: Copy of two Hill Cumorah scenes, Moroni, and Joseph Smith patterns (pages 11-12) on colored cardstock paper for each child, scissors, glue, and crayons

ACTIVITY: Create a Hill Cumorah scene with Moroni on one side burying the plates, and the Angel Moroni leading Joseph Smith to the plates on the other side.

1. Color and cut out two Hill Cumorah scenes: Moroni, and the Angel Moroni and Joseph patterns.
2. Fold both Hill Cumorah cards in half and cut slits where indicated.
3. Fold tab in on one side and glue Moroni burying plates on tab.
4. Fold tab in on other side and glue Angel Moroni guiding Joseph Smith to receive the plates on tab.
5. Glue Hill Cumorah scenes back to back.

THOUGHT TREAT: Golden Plate Cake. Bake a rectangle-shaped yellow cake. Frost with yellow-gold frosting. Write on half of the cake with Mormon's writings and the other half with Joseph's translation. Cut two 3" licorice strings and place them in the center of the cake. Place licorice strings on the cake to look like rings to hold the plates together.

BOOK OF MORMON: The Word of God

("Jerusalem" scene, obtaining the brass plates)

See lesson #17 in Primary 3-CTR B manual*.

YOU'LL NEED: Copy of the "Jerusalem" scene and figures (page 13-14) and the "Wilderness" scene and figures from Lesson #16 (pages 54-55) on colored cardstock paper for each child, scissors, and crayons

ACTIVITY: Review the story in 1 Nephi 1-2 from lesson #16 using the "Jerusalem" and "Wilderness" scenes and figures (pages 54-55). Then tell the story found in 1 Nephi 3-4 using the "Wilderness" and "Jerusalem" scenes and figures (pages 53-54) to create the story of Nephi and his brothers returning to Jerusalem to obtain the brass plates.

TO MAKE: Color and cut out "Jerusalem" scene, brass plates, Laban, Zoram, and angel figures. Use the "Wilderness" scene and figures from lesson #16 (Lehi, Sariah, Nephi, Laman, Lemuel, and Sam).

THOUGHT TREAT: Trail Mix. Mix together a granola, fruit and nut traveling trail mix in a sack children can munch on as they pretend they are traveling back to Jerusalem to obtain the brass plates.

*Primary 3-CTR B manual is published by The Church of Jesus Christ of Latter-day Saints, Salt Lake City, Utah.

Joseph Smith receives the plates.

Another Testament of Jesus Christ

Moroni buries the plates.

The Coming Forth of the Book of Mormon

*Primary 3-CTR B manual is published by The Church of Jesus Christ of Latter-day Saints, Salt Lake City, Utah.

*Primary 3-CTR B manual is published by The Church of Jesus Christ of Latter-day Saints, Salt Lake City, Utah.

C

CHOOSE THE RIGHT: I Will Follow Jesus

("Chews" the Right gum machine with glue-on stickers)   See lesson #1 in Primary 3-CTR B manual*.

YOU'LL NEED: Copy of gum ball machine and Thought Treat "Chews" the Right gum wrapper patterns (page 16) on cardstock paper gum balls, 3" stick of gum, and a zip-close plastic bag for each child, scissors, glue, and crayons

ACTIVITY: To help children make a promise to follow Heavenly Father by choosing the right. Create a gum ball machine to show ways you can "chews" the right.
1. Ahead of time, cut a slit in gum ball machine with a razor blade (to place CTR coin).
2. Color and cut out gum ball machine, CTR coin, and glue-on stickers.
3. Glue stickers on gum ball circles.
4. Insert CTR coin in money slot.

THOUGHT TREAT: "Chews" the Right Chewing Gum
Give child a piece of gum to chew (gum ball or wrapped gum, if it is not Fast Sunday). Option #1: A stick of gum can be inserted behind the CTR coin in the money slot in gum machine. Option #2: Place several gum balls inside a plastic bag and attach to the back of gum ball machine with double-stick tape.

CHRISTMAS: Jesus Christ Was Born on the Earth

(Samuel and Jesus star mobile ornament)   See lesson #47 in Primary 3-CTR B manual*.

YOU'LL NEED: Copy of star patterns (page 17) on colored cardstock paper and "10 piece of yarn for each child, scissors, paper punch, and crayons

ACTIVITY: Create a star and baby Jesus mobile to show the prophet Samuel the Lamanite and the angel announcing the birth of Jesus. Have children read Helaman 14:2, 5 and Luke 2:9-15 to compare the stories.
1. Color and cut out the star mobile pieces.
2. Fold both baby Jesus and star to make a two-sided ornament.
3. Glue together.
4. Punch a hole with a paper punch where indicated on the star and Jesus in a manger.
5. Tie yarn or ribbon through holes. Tie one from baby Jesus to the star and one on top of the star to hang mobile. This can be hung on the Christmas tree as an ornament.

THOUGHT TREAT: Christmas Star Cookie or Cookie Wall. Make a graham cracker sandwich (frost center). Hold sandwich up to look like a wall. Place a finger on the top of cookie to represent Samuel telling of Jesus coming.

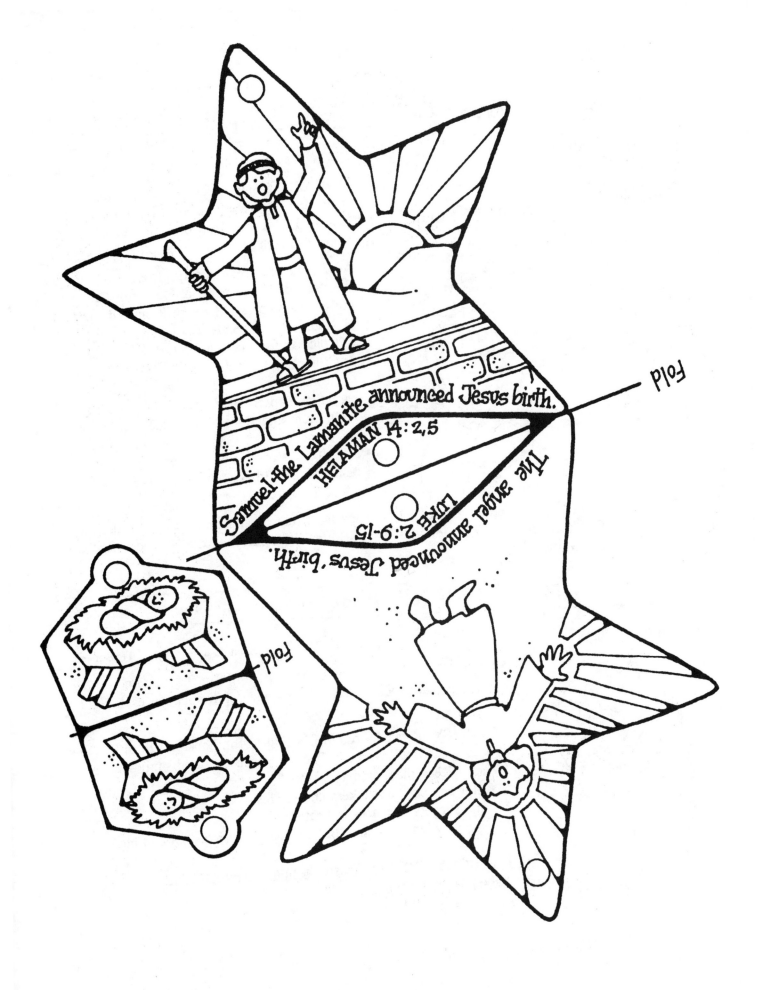

Fold

Samuel the Lamanite announced Jesus birth.

HELAMAN 14: 2,5

The angel announced Jesus birth.

LUKE 2:9-15

Fold

Fold

C

COMMANDMENTS: Heavenly Father Helps Us Obey

(Nephi's ship puzzle scene)

See lesson #18 in Primary 3-CTR B manual*.

YOU'LL NEED: Copy of ship pattern (page 19) on colored cardstock paper and an extra 8 1/2" x 11" sheet of light blue cardstock paper for each child, scissors, glue, and crayons

ACTIVITY: Create a ship puzzle scene to tell the story of Nephi obeying Heavenly Father by building a ship to sail to the Promised Land (1 Nephi 3:7; 17; 18:1-4).
1. Color and cut out ship puzzle pieces.
2. Glue-mount puzzle pieces to create a ship scene on an 8 1/2" x 11" sheet of light blue cardstock paper. Be sure to glue-mount only the bottom and sides of ship, leaving top open for a pocket.
3. Tell the story, using figures from pages 55 and 14 (Nephi and his family). Cut tabs off figures.

THOUGHT TREAT: Boat Treats. Option #1 Banana Boat (cut open a small banana and sprinkle miniature chocolate chips in center) Option #2 Peanut Butter Celery Boat (cut a 3" piece of celery and fill with peanut butter)

COMMANDMENTS Help Me Choose the Right

(feel good flip-flag)

See lesson #3 in Primary 3-CTR B manual*.

YOU'LL NEED: Copy of heart and smile flip-flag pattern (page 20) on colored cardstock paper and a wooden craft stick for each child, scissors, glue, and crayons

ACTIVITY: Create a round flip-flag to flip back and forth to show two images: Heart reads, "I Feel Good Inside," and smile reads, "When I Keep the Commandments."
1. Color and cut out stickers and circles.
2. Glue stickers in places indicated.
3. Glue wooden craft stick in between two circles back-to-back.

THOUGHT TREAT: Frosted round cookie with a heart shaped candy on top

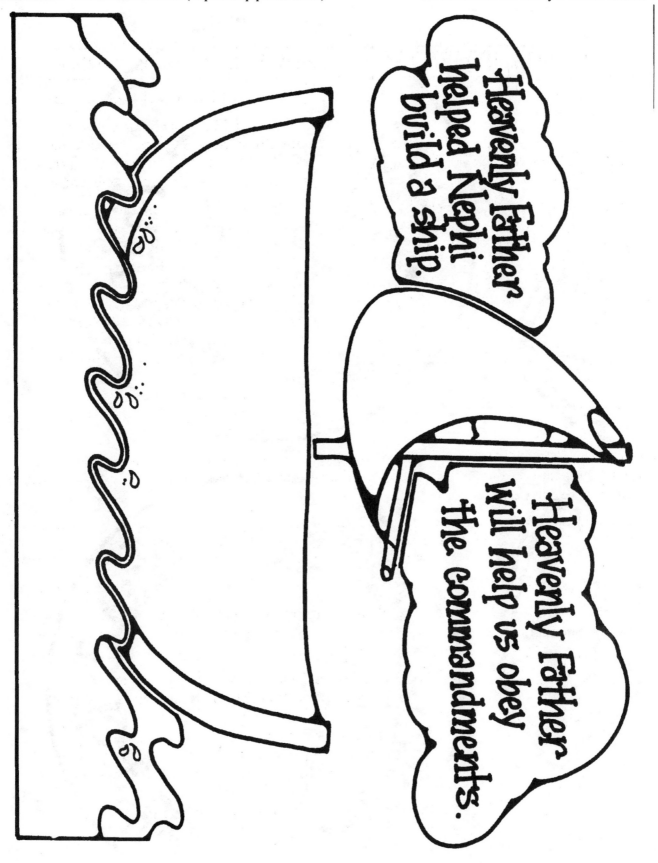

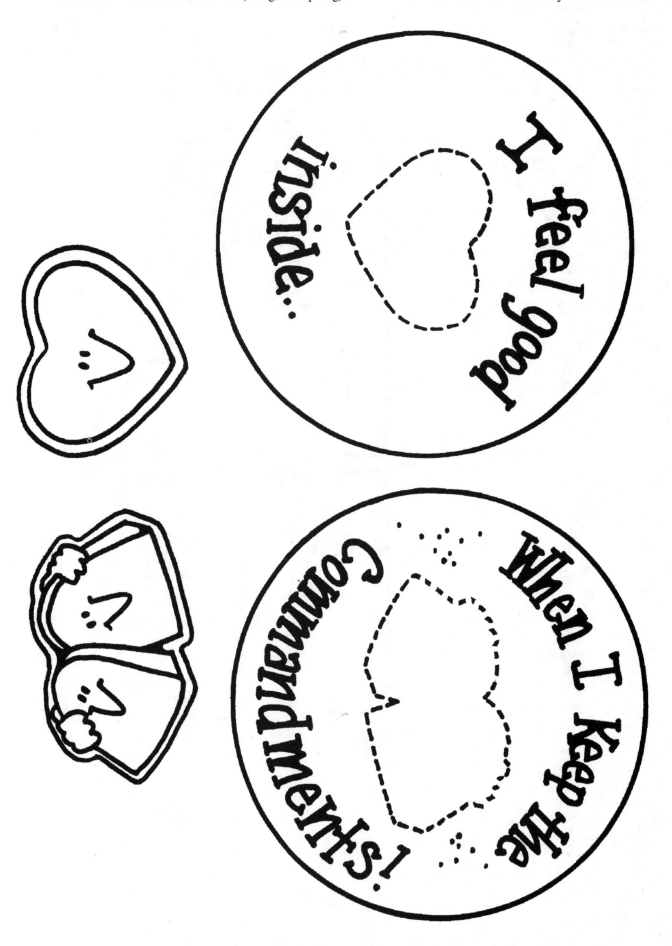

I feel good inside.

When I keep the Commandments!

    *Primary 3-CTR B manual is published by The Church of Jesus Christ of Latter-day Saints, Salt Lake City, Utah.

D-E

DO GOOD UNTO OTHERS

(Golden ruler)

See lesson #44 in Primary 3-CTR B manual*.

YOU'LL NEED: Copy of golden ruler parts A and B patterns (page 22) on colored cardstock paper for each child, scissors, glue or tape, and crayons

ACTIVITY: Help child learn ways to follow the Golden Rule: Do unto others as you would have them do unto you (Matthew 7:12, and Luke 6:31).
1. Color and cut out golden ruler parts A and B.
2. Tape or glue part B to the bottom of part A where indicated.
3. Encourage children to post this somewhere at home to remind them to do good unto others.

THOUGHT TREAT: Golden Ruler Wafer Cookies. Purchase yellow wafer cookies. Tell children that they will be happy when they follow the golden rule and do good unto others.

EASTER: I Can Live Forever with the Help of Jesus

(resurrection slide-show)

See lesson #46 in Primary 3-CTR B manual*.

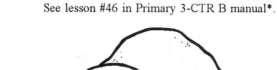

YOU'LL NEED: Copy of tomb, rock, and pull-through picture strip patterns (page 23) on colored cardstock paper and a metal or button brad for each child, razor blade (to use prior to activity), scissors, glue, and crayons

ACTIVITY: Create a resurrection pull-through picture strip to show the part Jesus played in the resurrection. Tell children that we can have our body forever because Jesus died and was resurrected for us.
1. Before activity, cut slits on both sides of tomb with a razor blade.
2. Color and cut out the tomb, rock, and pull-through picture strip.
3. Attach rock to side of tomb with a metal or button brad to open and close.
4. Slide (insert) picture strip into slips on sides of tomb. Bend tabs backwards to keep strip from sliding out.

To Make Button Brad: Sew two buttons together on opposite sides (threading thread through the same hole) to attach repentance wheels.

THOUGHT TREAT: Bread Rolls or Round Sugar Cookie to pretend rolling back the stone.

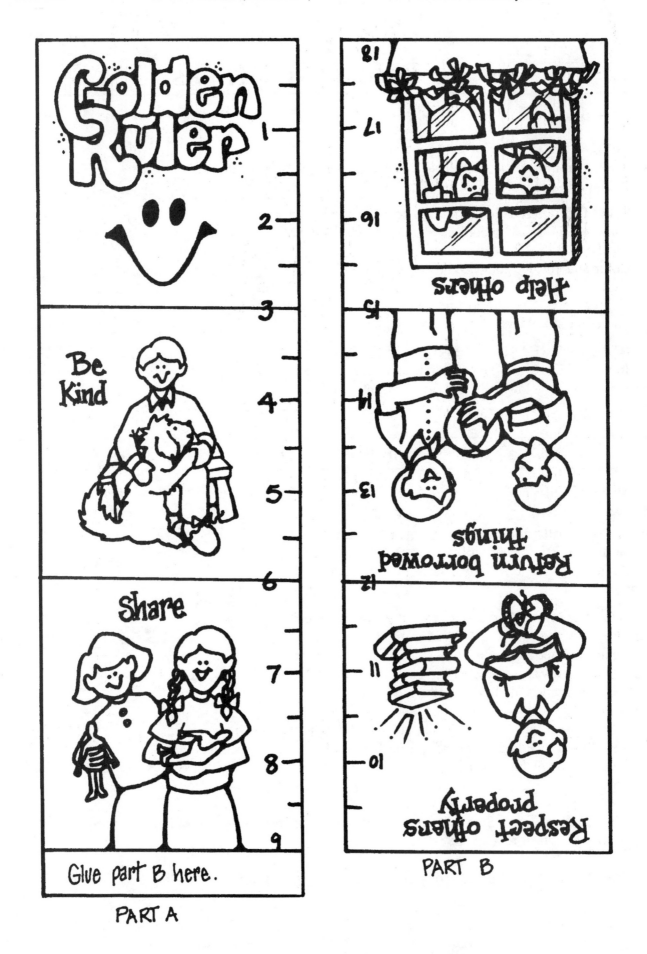

     *Primary 3-CTR B manual is published by The Church of Jesus Christ of Latter-day Saints, Salt Lake City, Utah.

PATTERN: EASTER (resurrection slide-show)   See lesson #46 in Primary 3-CTR B manual*.

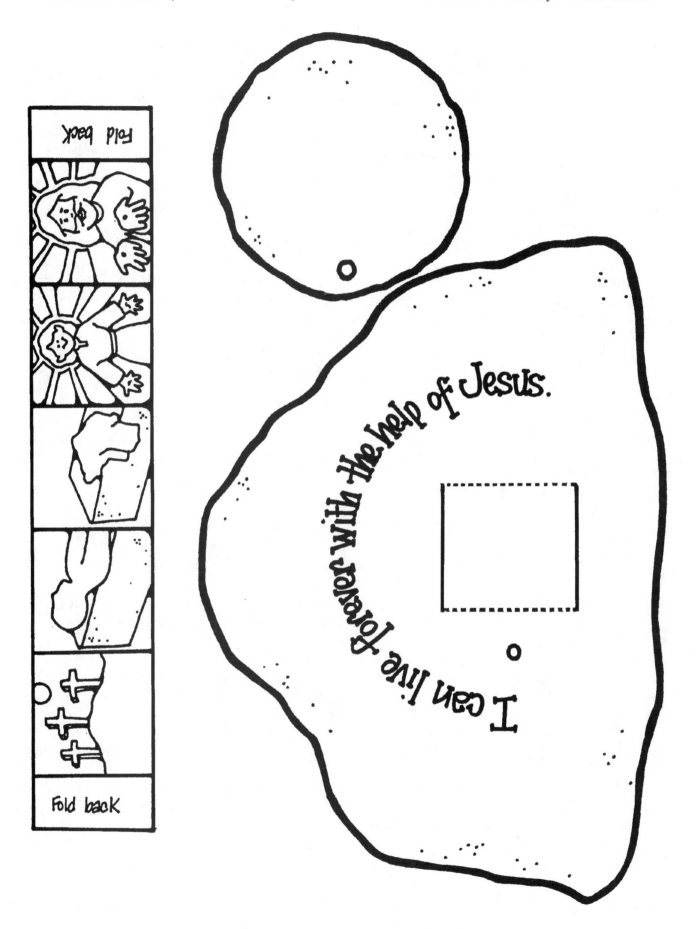

*Primary 3-CTR B manual is published by The Church of Jesus Christ of Latter-day Saints, Salt Lake City, Utah.

E-F

EXAMPLE: I Can Be a Good Example

(ice cream sundae poster with glue-on stickers)

See lesson #45 in Primary 3-CTR B manual*.

YOU'LL NEED: Copy of ice cream sundae bowl and ice cream patterns (page 25-26) on colored cardstock paper for each child, scissors, glue, and crayons

ACTIVITY: Help child learn ways to be a good example to their family.
1. Color and cut out ice cream bowl and ice cream scoops.
2. Glue ice cream scoops in bowl and say, "My life is full of flavor when I am a good example. We can scoop up good deeds daily."

THOUGHT TREAT: Ice cream sandwiches cut in half or bite-size ice cream treats (eat over table to avoid mess, and use wet-wipes or a wet cloth)

FAITH: I Can Live Forever with the Help of Jesus

("My Faith in Jesus Grows" seeds planted in a paper cup)

See lesson #29 in Primary 3-CTR B manual*.

YOU'LL NEED: Copy of label for planter pot pattern (page 27) on colored cardstock paper, and two 8-ounce paper cups, potting soil, and seeds for each child, scissors, glue or tape, and crayons

ACTIVITY: Create a pot to plant seeds in for each child to remind them that their faith in Jesus can grow. It starts as a small seed and grows into a testimony as they choose the right.
1. Color and cut out pot label.
2. Make a pot by placing two 8-ounce paper cups inside each other (for durability). Punch a small hole in the bottom for drainage.
3. Glue or tape label on cup.
4. Fill cup half way with potting soil, drop in seeds, and fill the other half with potting soil. Have children water plant when they get home.

THOUGHT TREAT: Fruit with Seeds. Show children the seeds that make the plant grow, i.e. apples, tangerines, kiwi, watermelon, and/or strawberries.

*Primary 3-CTR B manual is published by The Church of Jesus Christ of Latter-day Saints, Salt Lake City, Utah.

My life is full of flavor when I'm a good example.

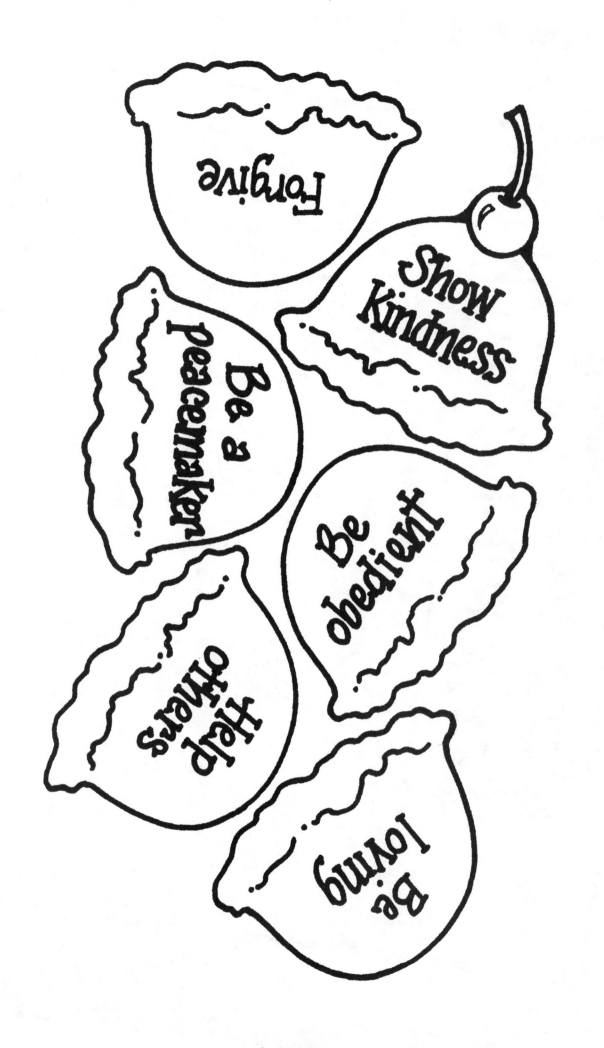

PATTERN: Faith
("My Faith in Jesus Grows"
paper cup label) to plant
seeds in paper cup

See lesson #29 in Primary
3-CTR B manual*.

Glue or tape here

My faith in
Jesus
Christ
can grow!

It will start
as a small
seed and
grow into a
testimony!

*Primary 3-CTR B manual
is published by The Church
of Jesus Christ of Latter-
day Saints, Salt Lake City,
Utah.

F

FAITH in Jesus Christ

("Jesus Is My Light" light switch cover)   See lesson #7 in Primary 3-CTR B manual*.

YOU'LL NEED: Copy light switch cover pattern (page 29) on colored cardstock paper for each child, scissors, razor blade, glue, and crayons

ACTIVITY: Help child know that Jesus is the light in their lives. He is the light of the world (Doctrine and Covenants 10:70).
1. Ahead of time cut out light switch center with a razor blade.
2. Color and cut out light switch cover.
3. Have child take light switch cover home and tape over their light switch (show them how).

THOUGHT TREAT: <u>Sun Light Sugar Cookie</u>. Make a round shaped sugar cookie. Before baking, use a knife to draw a mouth and tiny slits (sun rays) around the outer edge. Press M&M® candies in dough for eyes. Sprinkle yellow sugar on top before baking. To color sugar, mix sugar and a few drops of yellow food coloring in a bottle and shake.

FASTING: I Can Grow Closer to Heavenly Father and Jesus

(fasting tree with fruit glue-on stickers)   See lesson #41 in Primary 3-CTR B manual*.

YOU'LL NEED: Copy fasting tree pattern (pages 30-31) on colored cardstock paper for each child, scissors, glue, and crayons

ACTIVITY: Create a fasting tree and glue six fruit smiles to show that children can grow closer to Heavenly Father as they fast. Signs read: Fast Sunday can be a happy day. When I go without, I won't pout. When I think of the blessings I receive, I smile. I will pray for others when I fast. Heavenly Father is proud when I fast. My tummy is empty, but my spirit is full.
1. Color and cut out fasting tree and glue-on stickers.
2. Glue stickers in tree.
3. Have each child read or tell about how they can make fast day a happy day.

THOUGHT TREAT: If this is a fast Sunday, don't give treats. If not, give them each a bag of cereal to share with someone to show how they go without food to feed the poor and needy. Tell the story of the Good Samaritan who clothed and fed the hungry man who was beaten and left at the side of the road (Luke 10:30-34).

*Primary 3-CTR B manual is published by The Church of Jesus Christ of Latter-day Saints, Salt Lake City, Utah.

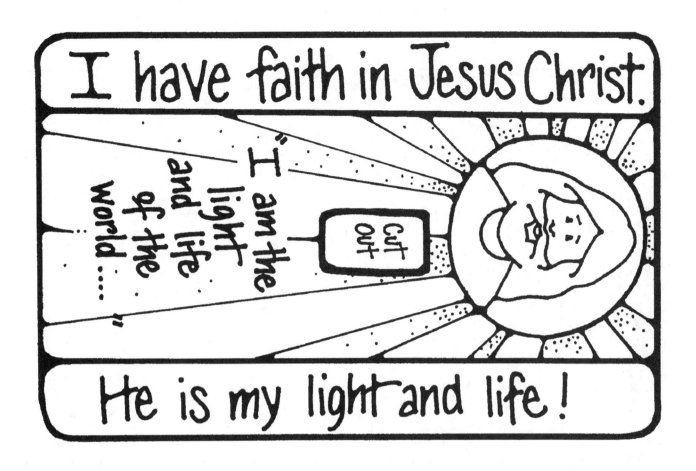

I can grow
close to Heavenly
Father when I fast.

FASTING TREE

PATTERN: FASTING (fasting tree with fruit glue-on stickers)   See lesson #41 in Primary 3-CTR B manual*.

F

FIRST VISION: Joseph Smith saw Heavenly Father and Jesus

(Sacred Grove movable scene)

See lesson #5 in Primary 3-CTR B manual*.

YOU'LL NEED: Copy of Sacred Grove scene with Heavenly Father and Jesus, and Joseph Smith patterns (page 33) on colored cardstock paper and page reinforcements (see #3 below), and 12" string for each child, scissors, glue. tape, and crayons

ACTIVITY: Learn of Joseph Smith who prayed in the grove of trees, and saw Heavenly Father and Jesus.
1. Color and cut out Sacred Grove scene, Joseph Smith, Heavenly Father and Jesus.
2. Glue Joseph Smith sticker in place.
3. Poke two holes with a pencil. Place page reinforcements over holes on back.
4. Thread a 12" string through holes and tie a knot in front.
5. Tape the knot on the back of Heavenly Father and Jesus image.
6. Pull Heavenly Father and Jesus images up and down.

THOUGHT TREAT: Sacred Grove Celery "Tree". Serve celery spears with vegetable dip.

FORGIVE: Commandment to Forgive, Forget, Forever, For Jesus

(four for's necklace)

See lesson #23 in Primary 3-CTR B manual*.

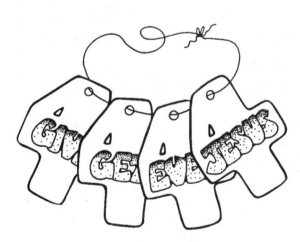

YOU'LL NEED: Copy four of the number "4" patterns (page 34) on colored cardstock paper, and 30" yarn or ribbon for each child, scissors, paper punch, and crayons

ACTIVITY: Heavenly Father and Jesus want us to forgive others for the wrong things they do to us. Create a necklace to remind them that we are to forgive, forget, forever, for Jesus.
1. Color and cut out the four number 4's.
2. Punch a hole at the top of each number.
3. Thread a 30" piece of yarn or ribbon through each and tie to child's neck.
4. Review what the necklace says, that we are to Forgive others and Forget, Forever, For Jesus.

THOUGHT TREAT: 4 Treats to Remember to Forgive, Forget, Forever, For Jesus. Treats could be 4 graham crackers or 4 pieces of candy.

*Primary 3-CTR B manual is published by The Church of Jesus Christ of Latter-day Saints, Salt Lake City, Utah.

PATTERN: FIRST VISION (Sacred Grove movable scene)   See lesson #5 in Primary 3-CTR B manual*.

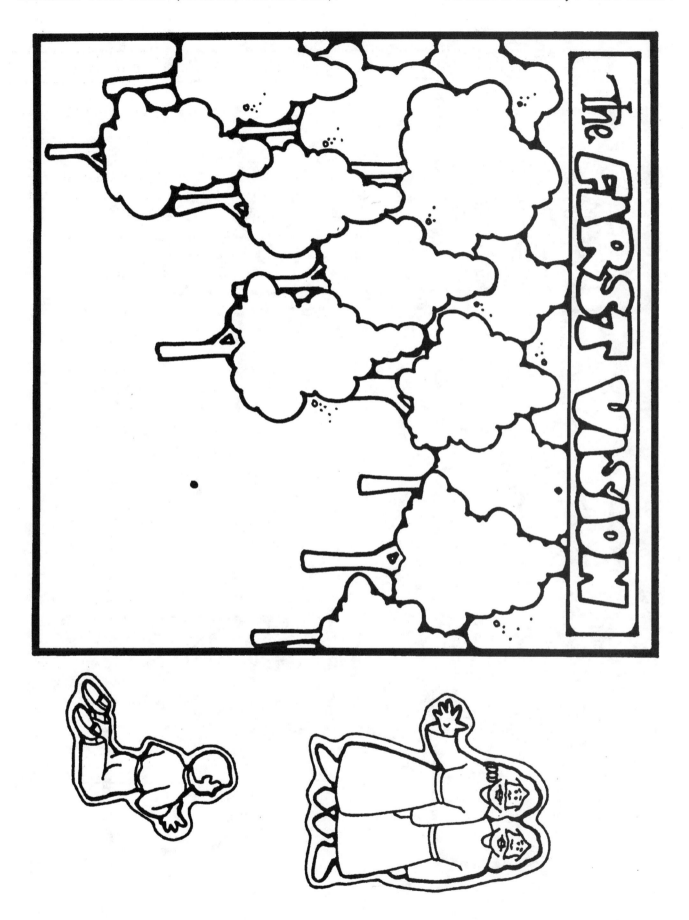

H

HEAVENLY FATHER'S PLAN: He Trusts Us to Follow His Plan

("Right Road to Heaven" road map with trusty truck)

See lesson #2 in Primary 3-CTR B manual*.

YOU'LL NEED: Copy of road map and trusty truck pattern (page 36) on colored cardstock paper for each child, scissors, glue, and crayons. Option: Two magnets for each child.

ACTIVITY: To help children show Heavenly Father that they can be trusted to make the right choices, create a "Right Road to Heaven" road map and follow it from the start (their earthly home) to heaven with their trusty truck. Road signs show the way back to Heavenly Father.

1. Color and cut out road map and trusty truck.
2. Place truck on path and show children the way back to their heavenly home. Option: Glue a magnet on the back of the trusty truck. Have another magnet to place on the back of road map to move trusty truck on the trail.

THOUGHT TREAT: Trusty Truck Wheels. Round wheel shaped hard candies. Children can have a "wheelie" good time eating and thinking how sweet it would be to live with Heavenly Father.

HOLY GHOST Guides Us to Know the Truth

(friendship necklace/medallion)

See lesson #20 in Primary 3-CTR B manual*.

YOU'LL NEED: Copy medallion pattern (page 37) on yellow cardstock paper, and 30" yarn or ribbon for each child, scissors, paper punch, glue, and glitter, and crayons

ACTIVITY: Create a medallion to remind each child that "The Holy Ghost is My Friend ... He's True and Honest to the End." The Holy Ghost gives them a special light when they choose the right.

1. Color, cut out, and decorate medallion with glitter.
2. Punch a hole at the top of medallion with paper punch.
3. Thread a piece of yarn or ribbon through hole and tie around child's neck.

THOUGHT TREAT: Happy Cookies (sugar cookie with a frosted or painted smile). Cookie Paint Recipe: Before baking cookie, paint smile face on cookie with cookie paint (mix two teaspoons canned milk with food coloring). Tell children that the Holy Ghost is their friend and can make them feel happy.

PATTERN:
HOLY GHOST
(friendship
necklace/medallion)

See lesson #20 in
Primary 3-CTR B
manual*.

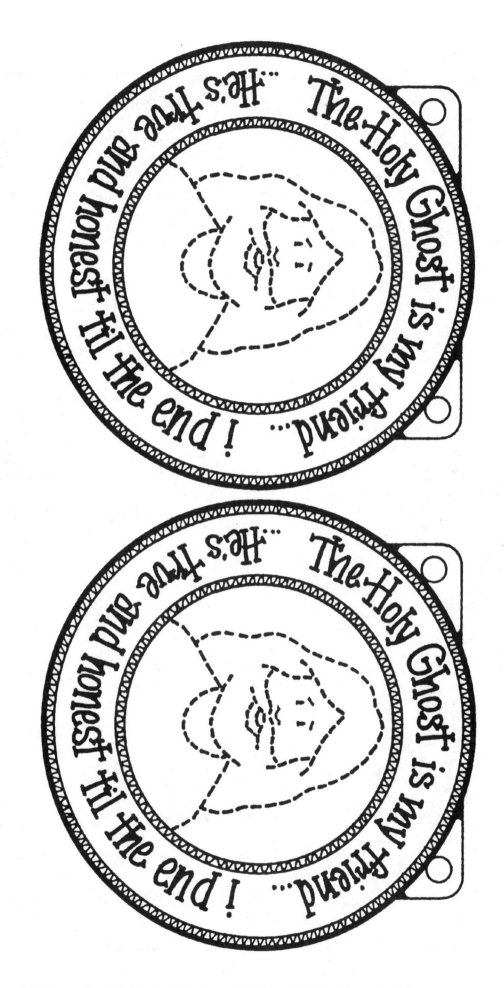

*Primary 3-CTR B manual is published by The Church of Jesus Christ of Latter-day Saints, Salt Lake City, Utah.

H

HOLY GHOST Helps Me

(headband and medallion)

See lesson #26 in Primary 3-CTR B manual*.

YOU'LL NEED: Copy of mind headband and heart medallion pattern (page 39) on colored cardstock paper, 30" yarn or ribbon for each child, scissors, paper punch, and crayons

ACTIVITY: Create a headband and medallion to show children how the Holy Ghost speaks to them.
  #1 Mind headband reads: "The Holy Ghost speaks to my mind. I listen and obey."
  #2 Heart medallion reads: "The Holy Ghost speaks to my heart. I have a warm feeling when he is near."

TO MAKE HEADBAND AND MEDALLION:
1. Color and cut out headband pieces and heart medallion.

2. To Make Headband: Fold tabs on ears and glue where indicated. Glue sides A and B to left and right side of headband and size to child's head.

3. To Make Medallion: Punch hole where indicated. Thread with 30" yarn or ribbon. Tie at end and slip on child's neck.

THOUGHT TREAT: Heart Shaped Cookies (reminding child that the Holy Ghost can dwell in your heart).

HOLY GHOST: The Greatest Gift

(gift box)

See lesson #12 in Primary 3-CTR B manual*.

YOU'LL NEED: Copy box, Holy Ghost, and heart pocket (page 40) on colored cardstock paper for each child, scissors, glue, and crayons

ACTIVITY: Remind children that when they are eight (8) they can be baptized and receive the gift of the Holy Ghost. Create a gift box that shows the Holy Ghost inside a heart pocket. This will remind children that the Holy Ghost is a special gift that helps them to choose the right.

1. Color and cut out box, Holy Ghost, and heart pocket.

2. Fold corners of box and tabs.

3. Glue bottom of heart where indicated leaving top open for pocket, to slide in Holy Ghost.

4. Glue tabs on corners to make box. Fold bow forward to stand up on box.

THOUGHT TREAT: Lemon Jello® Jigglers® (gelatin squares)

*Primary 3-CTR B manual is published by The Church of Jesus Christ of Latter-day Saints, Salt Lake City, Utah.

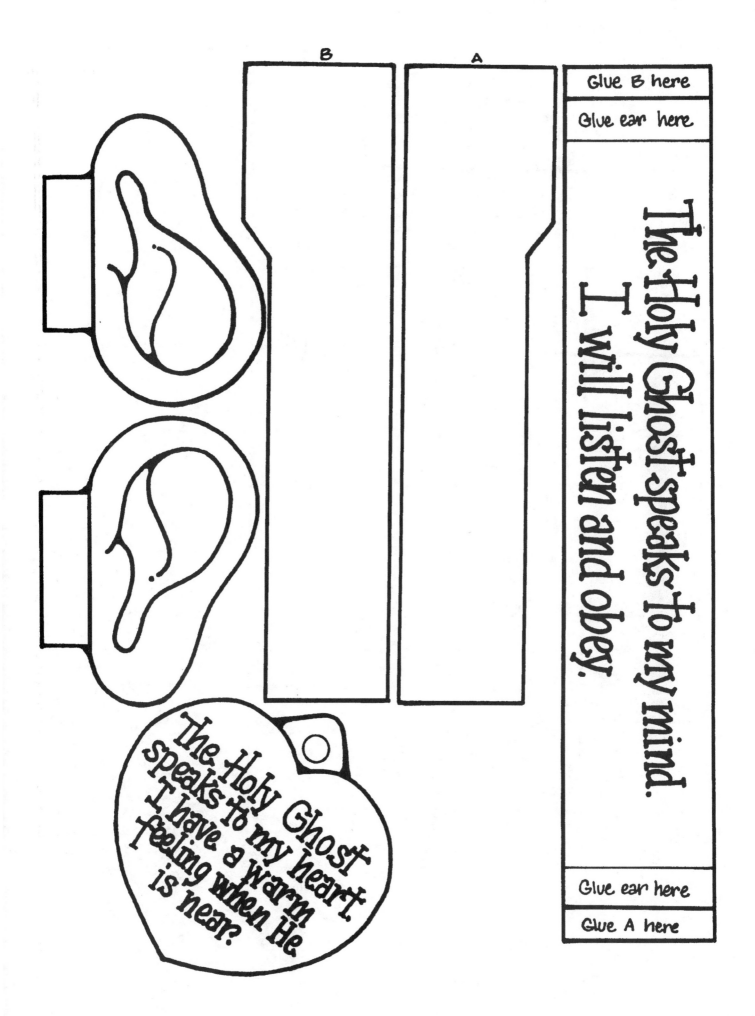

B

A

Glue B here

Glue ear here

The Holy Ghost speaks to my mind.
I will listen and obey.

Glue ear here

Glue A here

The Holy Ghost speaks to my heart.
I have a warm feeling when He is near?

See lesson #12 in Primary 3-CTR B manual*.

Fold forward

Fold back

The Greatest Gift

I can't wait until I'm 8!

To comfort, teach and help me obey.

I can recieve a special gift.

glue here

glue here

The Holy Ghost can be with me!

The Holy Ghost doesn't have a body, but he can dwell in my heart.

H-J

HONORING Names of Heavenly Father and Jesus

(reverent mouth pop-up picture)

See lesson #43 in Primary 3-CTR B manual*.

YOU'LL NEED: Copy of face with mouth piece pattern (page 42) on flesh colored cardstock paper for each child, scissors, glue, and crayons

ACTIVITY: Create a "I will speak" face with pop-up mouth that flaps over the words "... the names of Heavenly Father and Jesus Christ reverently." Pop-up mouth will remind child to honor the sacred names of Heavenly Father and Jesus Christ.
1. Have child draw their own hair to personalize picture.
2. Color and cut out face and mouth piece.
3. Cut a slit in the mouth where indicated for each child.
4. Stick the mouth piece through the slit. Fold and glue down mouth piece tab on the back side of the face.
5. Show children how to flap mouth up and down, helping them memorize the verse.

THOUGHT TREAT: <u>Lip Shaped Gelatin Blocks</u>. Create the Jell-o® Jigglers™ gelatin snacks recipe which requires 2 large (6 oz.) packages of Jell-o® (approximately 2 1/2 cups boiling water for 2 (6 oz.) packages of flavored gelatin). Pour into a 13" x 9" pan and chill three hours. Warm the bottom of pan with warm water to release. Cut out mouth shapes.

JOSEPH SMITH'S Childhood

(two-sided puzzle)

See lesson #4 in Primary 3-CTR B manual*.

YOU'LL NEED: Copy of two-sided puzzle pattern (page 43) on cardstock paper, an envelope or zip-close plastic bag to store puzzle pieces for each child, scissors, glue, and crayons

ACTIVITY: Imagine what the boy Joseph Smith would be like as you create and put together a puzzle that describes our Prophet Joseph Smith as a boy, i.e. had blue eyes, was born December 23.
1. Color picture.
2. Fold puzzle in half on dividing line back-to-back.
3. Glue picture side to word side (spreading glue over the entire piece, not just the edges).
4. Trim edges. Cut puzzle shapes out as shown on one side.
5. Place puzzle in an envelope or plastic bag for child to take home.

THOUGHT TREAT: <u>Gingerbread Boy</u> (thinking about Joseph Smith as a boy)

I will speak...

...the names of Heavenly Father and Jesus Christ reverently.

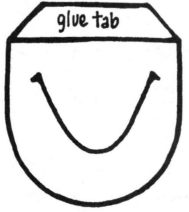

glue tab

*Primary 3-CTR B manual is published by The Church of Jesus Christ of Latter-day Saints, Salt Lake City, Utah.

PATTERN: JOSEPH SMITH (two-sided puzzle)   See lesson #4 in Primary 3-CTR B manual*.

L

LOVE: I Can Show Love for Jesus

(word picture story with glue-on stickers)   See lesson #36 in Primary 3-CTR B manual*.

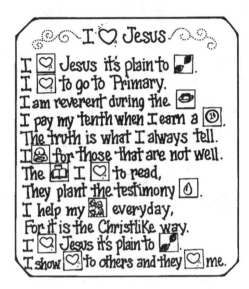

YOU'LL NEED: Copy of word picture story with glue-on stickers patterns (page 45) on colored cardstock paper for each child, scissors, glue, and crayons

ACTIVITY: Create a word picture story with picture glue-on stickers to learn ways to show love for Jesus by doing what he wants them to do.
1. Color and cut out word picture story and glue-on sticker pictures.
2. Match sticker pictures and glue them on word picture story.
3. Read the story together and think about how you can show love for Jesus.

THOUGHT TREAT: Heart-shaped Cookies

LOVE: Jesus Loves Us

("Thank you" people pop-ups)   See lesson #30 in Primary 3-CTR B manual*.

YOU'LL NEED: Copy of world and six people from different countries patterns (pages 46-47) on colored cardstock paper for each child, scissors, glue, and crayons

ACTIVITY: To show that Jesus loves and blesses all children, create a world with six different "Thank you" pockets, and people from different countries to slide down in pockets. Children can try to match the different people to the country where each language is spoken.
Country/Languages: German: *wir danken dir*, Danish: *tak*, Tongan: *malo*, French: *merci*, Japanese: *kansha shimashu*, Spanish: *gracias*.
1. Color and cut out world.
2. To create pockets, fold world in half and glue on both sides and along both dotted lines, leaving open 3 areas for child to insert people.
3. Have children guess which "thank you" goes with which country, sliding the person down in the pocket.

THOUGHT TREAT: Gingerbread Cookies (boys and girls)

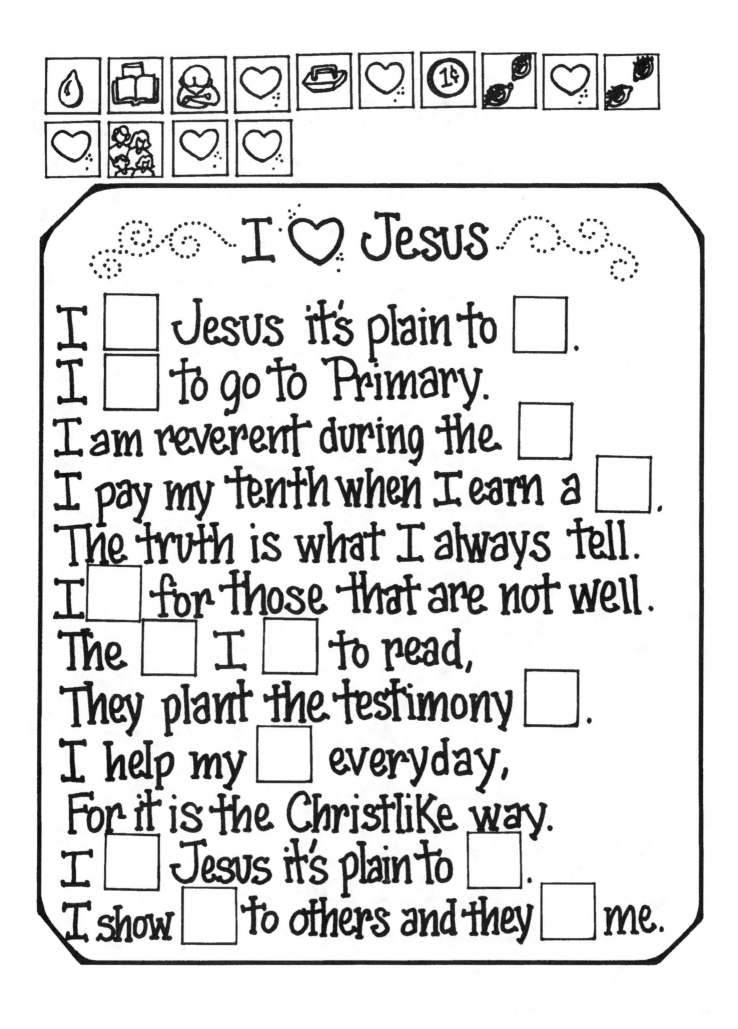

I ♡ Jesus

I ☐ Jesus it's plain to ☐.
I ☐ to go to Primary.
I am reverent during the ☐.
I pay my tenth when I earn a ☐.
The truth is what I always tell.
I ☐ for those that are not well.
The ☐ I ☐ to read,
They plant the testimony ☐.
I help my ☐ everyday,
For it is the Christlike way.
I ☐ Jesus it's plain to ☐.
I show ☐ to others and they ☐ me.

    *Primary 3-CTR B manual is published by The Church of Jesus Christ of Latter-day Saints, Salt Lake City, Utah.

*Primary 3-CTR B manual is published by The Church of Jesus Christ of Latter-day Saints, Salt Lake City, Utah.

L-M

LOVE: Jesus Wants Us to Love Everyone

(chain necklace with heart medallion)   See lesson #31 in Primary 3-CTR B manual*.

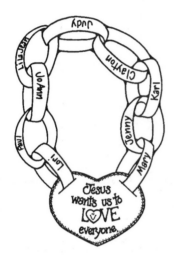

YOU'LL NEED: Copy of chains and heart medallion patterns (page 49) on colored cardstock paper, and 30" of yarn or ribbon for each child, scissors, glue, paper punch, and crayons

ACTIVITY: Create a chain necklace with a heart medallion to remind children that it is important to help others and that every child is of eternal worth to Heavenly Father and Jesus.

1. Color and cut out chains and heart medallion.
2. Write names of people you love. These could be the names of everyone in your Primary class or own family members.
3. Fold chains looping them inside each other and taping them closed.
4. Punch two holes in the heart medallion.
5. Thread chains through heart slip where indicated.
6. Place around child's neck.

THOUGHT TREAT: Cereal Necklace with Heart Candy Center

MISSIONARIES: The Lord Helps Missionaries

(two-sided, hinged missionary dolls)   See lesson #24 in Primary 3-CTR B manual*.

YOU'LL NEED: Copy of Ammon (Alma 17-19) and missionary of today body patterns (pages 50-51) on colored cardstock paper, and five metal or button brads for each child, scissors, glue, and crayons

ACTIVITY: Children create a set of two-sided, hinged missionary dolls to show how we can be like Ammon who was a good missionary. Jesus helps missionaries teach others about his Church. Ammon was a good servant who protected the king's sheep. Ammon had a strong testimony of Jesus Christ. Ammon knew that the spirit would help him teach King Lamoni. King Lamoni trusted Ammon and listened as Ammon told him about the gospel of Jesus Christ.

1. Color and cut out Ammon and Lamoni body parts.
2. Glue doll parts back-to-back this way: Don't glue top of arms, legs, and neck, as body parts need to move freely. Glue hands together (not arm), feet together (not legs), and top of heads together (not neck).

3. Attach body parts to body with metal or button brads. To Make Button Brad: Sew two buttons together on opposite sides (threading thread through the same hole) to attach body parts.
4. Read message on dolls.
5. Have children role play with their doll if time allows.

THOUGHT TREAT: Missionary M&M's. Purchase M&M® candies and give children two at a time to eat telling them that when missionaries go out today they go in twos to preach the gospel of Jesus Christ.

*Primary 3-CTR B manual is published by The Church of Jesus Christ of Latter-day Saints, Salt Lake City, Utah.

Ammon had a strong testimony of Jesus Christ. He knew that the spirit would help him teach King Lamoni.

Alma 17-19

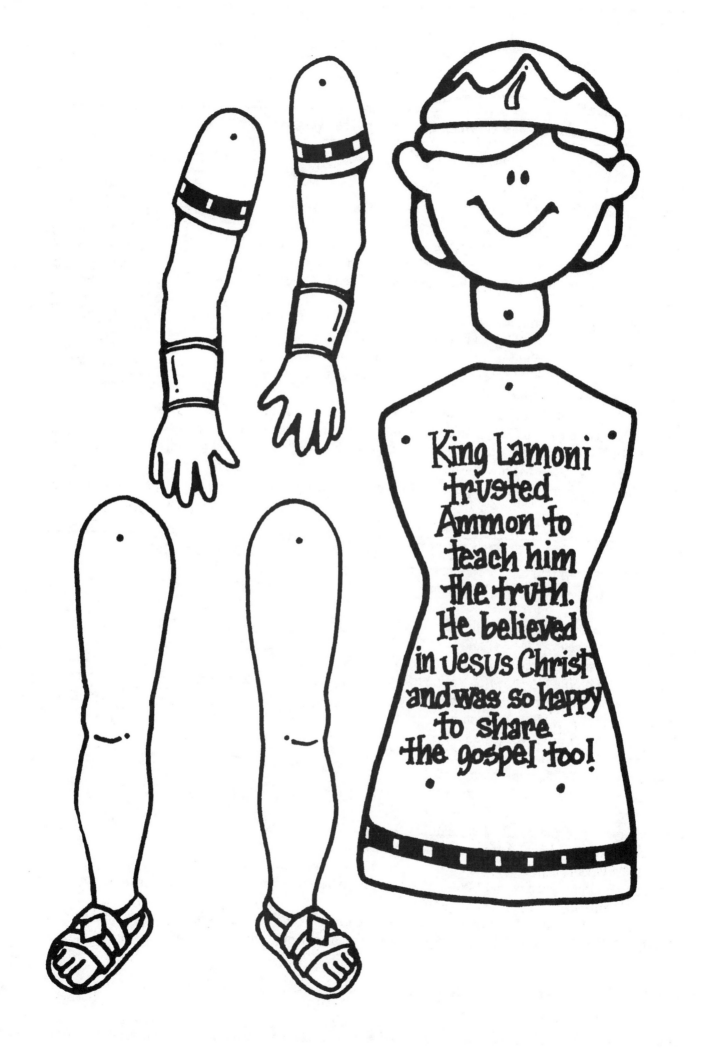

King Lamoni
trusted
Ammon to
teach him
the truth.
He believed
in Jesus Christ
and was so happy
to share
the gospel too!

M-O

MISSIONARY: I Can Do Missionary Work Now

(missionary savings bank) See lesson #25 in Primary 3-CTR B manual*.

YOU'LL NEED: Copy of can label pattern (page 53) on colored cardstock paper and a 10 3/4 oz. can containing Campbells® broth for each child, scissors, glue, and crayons

ACTIVITY: Children can start saving for and doing missionary work now. Create a missionary savings bank that they can't open until their mission. The bank on their dresser will remind them of missionary work.

Ahead of Time: Punch a hole in the top of a Campbells® 10 3/4 oz. can of broth (not soup). Use a knife to punch hole in the can the width of a quarter so children can drop money into the bank (soup can). Drain broth from soup can and rinse broth out of can with water. Remove label from can.

With Children: Color and cut out can label. Glue or tape label on can.

First Coin: Give each child a coin to drop into mission savings bank.

THOUGHT TREAT: Missionary Munchies. Missionaries love to receive snacks in the mail, like popcorn and cookies. Make your favorite munchies to share with children and send to a missionary. Place them in a box in a bed of popcorn to prevent breakage. Or, send Rice Krispies Treats® (see Kellogg's® cereal box).

OBEDIENCE: Be Obedient to Show Faith

("Wilderness" scene, leaving Jerusalem) See lesson #16 in Primary 3-CTR B manual*.

YOU'LL NEED: Copy of both the "Wilderness" scene (page 54) and the "Jerusalem" scene from lesson #17 (page 13) and figure patterns (page 55) on colored cardstock paper for each child, scissors, and crayons. **COPY AHEAD** lesson #17 figures (page 14) to use next week.

ACTIVITY: Tell the story found in 1 Nephi 1-2 using the "Wilderness" scene and "Jerusalem" scenes and the figures on page 55) to create the story of Lehi who obeyed Heavenly Father and Jesus. Lehi and his family left the beautiful city of Jerusalem and went into the wilderness to find safety.

1. Color and cut out city and "Wilderness" and "Jerusalem" scene, Lehi, Sariah, Nephi, Laman, Lemuel, and Sam.

2. Place family first in "Jerusalem" scene and then in the "Wilderness" scene to tell of their journey.

THOUGHT TREAT: Wilderness Snacks. Create a trail mix with dried fruit, seeds, and nuts.

PATTERN: MISSIONARY
(missionary savings bank)

See lesson #25 in
Primary 3-CTR B manual*.

PATTERN: OBEDIENCE (Lehi and his family)

See lesson #16 in Primary 3-CTR B manual*.

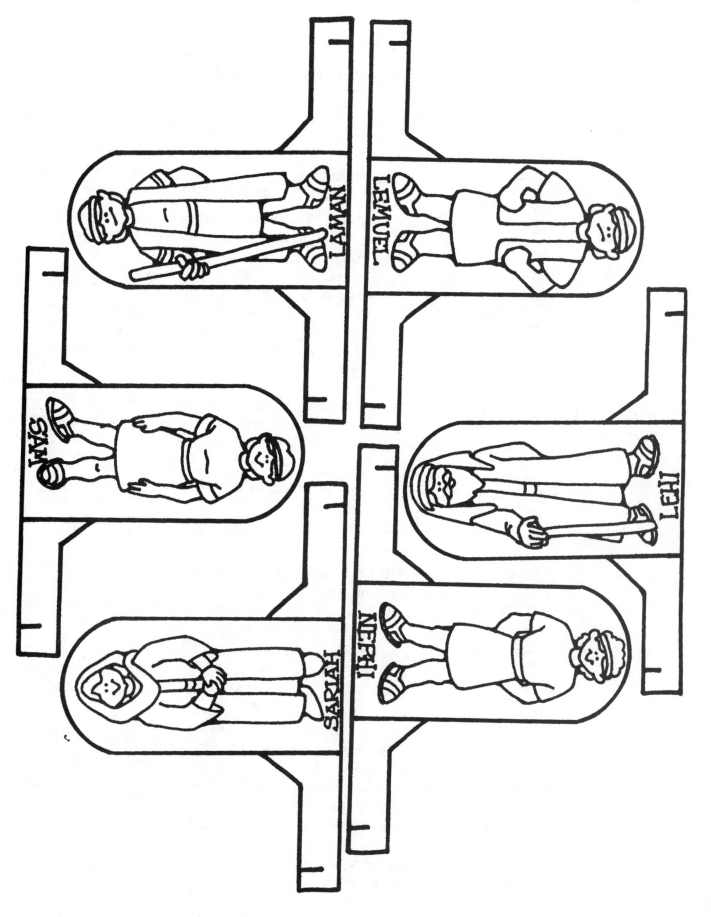

*Primary 3-CTR B manual is published by The Church of Jesus Christ of Latter-day Saints, Salt Lake City, Utah.

P

PARENTS: My Parents Help Me Learn

(slide-show)

See lesson #28 in Primary 3-CTR B manual*.

YOU'LL NEED: Copy of home and pull-through pictures (page 57) on colored cardstock paper for each child, scissors, glue, razor blade, and crayons

ACTIVITY: Show children ways their parents help them learn to obey the commandments with pull-through pictures.
1. Ahead of time, cut out slits on both sides of door with a razor blade.
2. Color and cut out home and pull-through pictures.
3. Insert or slide through pictures
4. Fold back edges of picture to prevent pulling all the way out.

THOUGHT TREAT: Graham Cracker House. Create a house for each child. Frost four small graham crackers on sides (sticking sides together) to make a house. Talk about the children's house and what they learn inside the house, and how they obey the commandments.

PARENTS: I Can Show Love to My Parents by "Bee"ing O"bee"dient

(O"bee"diance meter)

See lesson #39 in Primary 3-CTR B manual*.

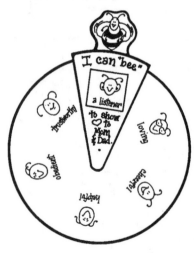

YOU'LL NEED: Copy of obedience wheel and "I Can 'Bee' Obedient" meter patterns (page 58) on colored cardstock paper, and a metal or button brad for each child, razor blade, scissors, glue, and crayons

ACTIVITY: Using the o"bee"diance meters, show children ways they can show love to their parents by being obedient.
1. Ahead of time, cut out bee meter window with a razor blade.
2. Color and cut out wheel and bee meter.
3. Punch a hole in wheel and bee meter and attach a metal or button brad. To Make Button Brad: Sew two buttons together on opposite sides (threading thread through the same hole) to attach bee meter to wheel.
4. Turn wheel and talk about each way you can show obedience to parents.

THOUGHT TREAT: Honey Bee Bread. Whip honey with butter (equal amounts) to create honey butter to spread on bread. Remind them that honey is sweet, and it is sweet of them to obey their parents.

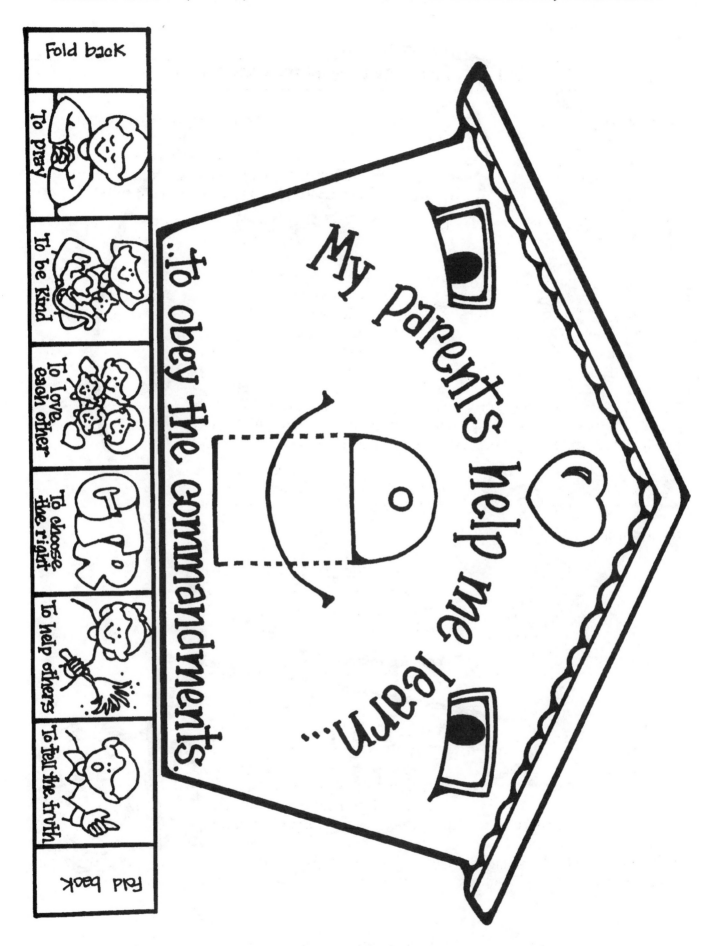

Fold back

To pray

To be kind

To love each other

To choose the right

To help others

To tell the truth

Fold back

...to obey the commandments.

My parents help me learn...

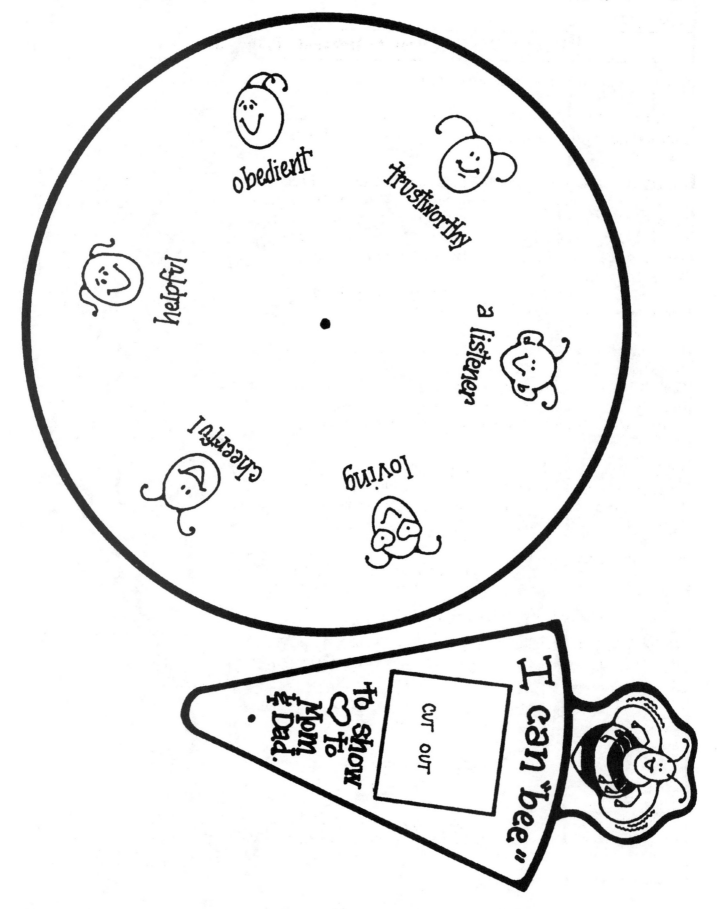

*Primary 3 -CTR B manual is published by The Church of Jesus Christ of Latter-day Saints, Salt Lake City, Utah.

P

PRAY: We Can Pray to Heavenly Father and Jesus

(Monday through Sunday prayer elevator)   See lesson #34 in Primary 3-CTR B manual*.

YOU'LL NEED: Copy of paper doll child praying and elevator pattern (page 60) on colored cardstock paper, scissors, glue, tape, and crayons

ACTIVITY: To encourage children to pray to Heavenly Father as Jesus did, create an elevator where child can pray each day, Monday - Sunday. Child pulls the string or ribbon to pull the paper doll child up the elevator seven times (once daily) to get the full message written on the fan: "I grow each day when I pray ... closer to Heavenly Father."
1. Color and cut out elevator, child praying, and wordstrip.
2. Glue head on wordstrip where indicated.
3. Cut slits in top and bottom of the elevator.
4. Thread strip through top and bottom slits in elevator with head at the top.
5. Tape or glue strip ends together where indicated so strip will move freely.
6. Move child arrow to first day, then down to reveal message at the end of the week.

THOUGHT TREAT: Monday-Sunday Mints. Give each child 7 small butter mints one at a time. As mints melt in their mouth ask them to say the days of the week. Then say, "Heavenly Father and Jesus wants us ("mint" for us) to pray every day of the week Monday, Tuesday, Wednesday - Sunday."

PRAYER: Heavenly Father Helps Us When We Pray

(Jesus praying in the Garden dot-to-dot)   See lesson #19 in Primary 3-CTR B manual*.

YOU'LL NEED: Copy of Jesus praying dot-to-dot pattern (page 61) on colored cardstock paper, and a pencil for each child, and crayons

ACTIVITY: Create a dot-to-dot picture of Jesus praying in the Garden of Gethsemane to show that Jesus prayed to Heavenly Father for help because he loves us. Heavenly Father will help us when we pray.
1. Follow numbered dots to complete the picture.
2. Color picture.

THOUGHT TREAT: Frosted Sugar Cookies decorated with dots (red hot candies or decorator candies), or just use heart shaped candies.

Elevator Prayer Chart

Sunday
Monday
Tuesday
Wednesday
Thursday
Friday
Saturday

Glue B here

I grow each day when I pray to Heavenly Father.

Glue A here

A
B

A
B

*Primary 3-CTR B manual is published by The Church of Jesus Christ of Latter-day Saints, Salt Lake City, Utah.

Heavenly Father helps me when I pray.

P

PRIESTHOOD Blessings and Ordinances

(spiral kite to fly in the wind)

See lesson #9 in Primary 3-CTR B manual*.

YOU'LL NEED: Copy of spiral kite pattern (page 63) on colored cardstock paper, and 12" yarn or ribbon for each child, scissors, and crayons

ACTIVITY: To help children know that the priesthood is a special power to give blessings and perform ordinances such as baptism, and healing of the sick. Create a spiral kite that tells of this power. Take hold of string and move arms to watch spiral kite twirl.
1. Color and cut out spiral kite.
2. Poke a hole in the center spot indicated.
3. Tie 12" yarn or ribbon through hole and fly!

THOUGHT TREAT: Kite Cookies. Create sugar cookies in kite shapes (round-spiral). Frost and decorate with licorice strings and candies.

PROPHETS The Church Has Prophets to Teach Us

(make a prophet poster)

See lesson #8 in Primary 3-CTR B manual*.

YOU'LL NEED: Copy of prophet poster and clothes, hair, and face sticker patterns (pages 64-65) on flesh-colored cardstock paper for each child, scissors, clear contact paper, removable tape, and crayons

ACTIVITY: Create a prophet poster without a face or hair for each child to add clothes, hair and face tape on stickers to create a prophet from the Old Testament, Book of Mormon, or a modern-day prophet. Prophets might be Adam, Enoch, Noah, Abraham, Moses, Samuel, Jonah, Daniel, Lehi, or Nephi.
1. Color and cut out clothes, hair, and face tape-on stickers.
2. Place tape on back to double-stick to sticker and to prophet poster.
3. Create a prophet by taping stickers on face, hair, and body.
4. Have child tell what they know about the prophet they create.
OPTION: Color poster and laminate poster before. After poster pieces are colored, laminate with clear contact paper for durability.

THOUGHT TREAT: Prophet Face Cookie. Frost and decorate a round sugar cookie with coconut hair (mix orange and green food coloring in a bag with coconut to color coconut brown), candies for face and ears.

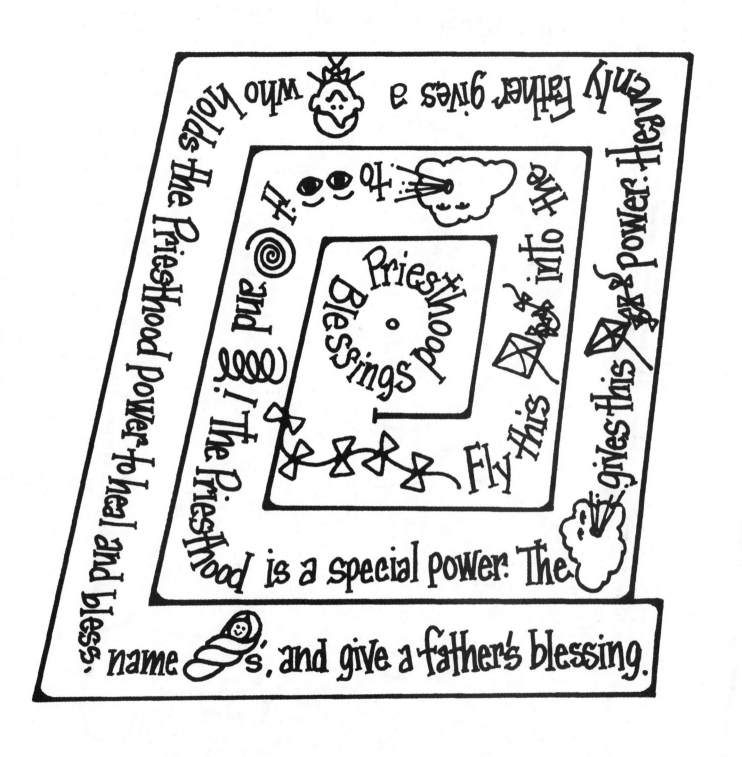

*Primary 3-CTR B manual is published by The Church of Jesus Christ of Latter-day Saints, Salt Lake City, Utah.

PORTRAIT OF A

PROPHET

PATTERN: PROPHET (make a prophet poster)

See lesson #8 in Primary 3-CTR B manual*.

*Primary 3-CTR B manual is published by The Church of Jesus Christ of Latter-day Saints, Salt Lake City, Utah.

P-R

PURE & RIGHTEOUS: I Will Think, Say, and Do as Jesus Did

("Jesus is my hero" doorknob sign)   See lesson #38 in Primary 3-CTR B manual*.

YOU'LL NEED: Copy of doorknob sign and glue-on word sticker patterns (page 67) on colored cardstock paper for each child, scissors, glue, and crayons

ACTIVITY: Create a "Jesus is my hero" doorknob sign to help children want to be pure and righteous as Jesus was. Tell children that Jesus has done more for us than any other person who has ever lived. He has saved us from death and made it possible for us to repent of our sins and be forgiven. We can be pure and righteous like Jesus. We can follow his example.
1. Color and cut out doorknob sign.
2. Have children place their sign on their door and say each day: "I will: think what Jesus would think, say what Jesus would say, and do what Jesus would do."

THOUGHT TREAT: "CTR" Sandwich. Stack three small graham crackers on top of each other with frosting between two layers. Write "CTR" on top with a frosting tube: To make tube, place 2 tablespoons frosting inside a plastic bag. Cut a hole in the corner and squeeze frosting through tube to write "CTR." Tell children that Jesus taught us how to Choose The Right. He is our hero. Let's Choose The Right so we can be like Him.

REPENTANCE Heals

(repentance bandage breastplate)   See lesson #10 in Primary 3-CTR B manual*.

YOU'LL NEED: Copy of bandage breastplate and glue-on sticker patterns (page 68) on colored cardstock paper, and 25" piece of yarn or ribbon for each child, scissors, paper punch, and crayons
OPTION: Decorate each bandage breastplate with a small bandage.

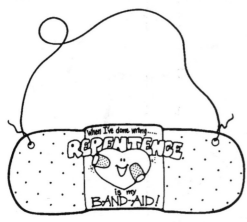

ACTIVITY:
1. Color and cut out repentance bandage breastplate and glue-on stickers.
2. Punch a hole on each side.
3. Tie end of ribbon or string in left and right holes.
4. Hang around child's neck and over chest.
OPTION: Place a small bandage on breastplate to decorate.

THOUGHT TREAT: Bandage Gum. You'll find novelty gum in the candy section. As children open gum and chew ask them to say, "When I've done wrong, repentance is my band-aid! I 'chew's to repent."

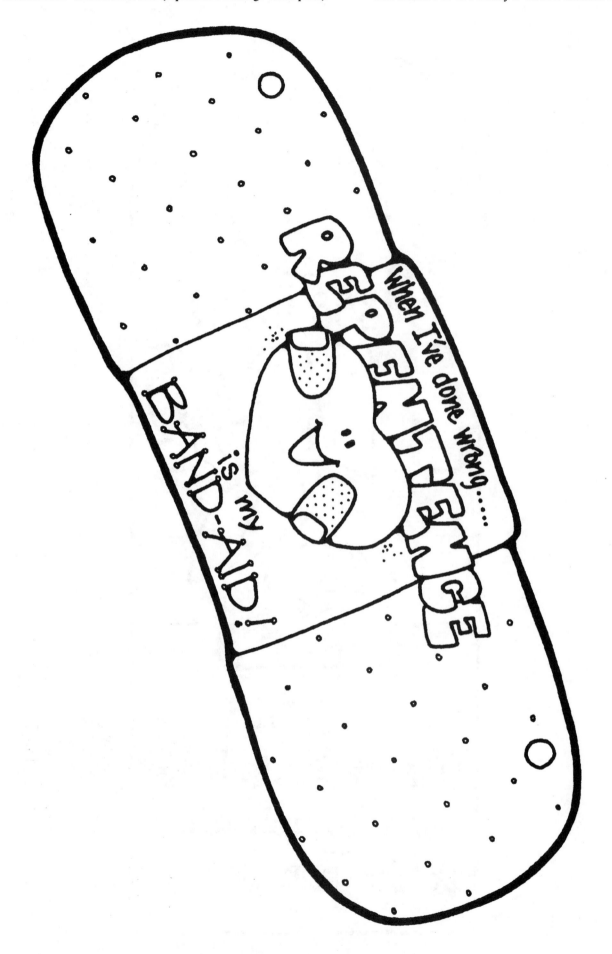

      *Primary 3-CTR B manual is published by The Church of Jesus Christ of Latter-day Saints, Salt Lake City, Utah.

R-S

RESTORATION: Jesus Christ's Church Restored

(membership window wheel)

See lesson #6 in Primary 3-CTR B manual*.

YOU'LL NEED: Copy of window wheel pattern (pages 70-71) on colored cardstock paper, and a metal or button brad for each child, scissors, and crayons

ACTIVITY: To show reasons why a child wants to be a member of The Church of Jesus Christ of Latter-day Saints.
1. Color and cut out wheel parts A and B.
2. Attach part A on top of part B with a metal or button brad. To Make Button Brad: Sew two buttons together on opposite sides (threading thread through the same hole) to attach window wheels.

THOUGHT TREAT: Graham Cracker Church. Break graham crackers into four pieces. Frost each corner to make a square building. Talk about building as Jesus Christ's church a long time ago. Then tear it down and say after Jesus left the church fell. Then when Joseph Smith came he restored the church or brought it back on the earth. Build another graham cracker church for each child to eat. Read the wheel "I want to be a member of The Church of Jesus Christ of Latter-day Saints because I can ..."

SACRAMENT: Remembering Jesus

(Last Supper shadow box)

See lesson #32 in Primary 3-CTR B manual*.

YOU'LL NEED: Copy of Last Supper shadow box, Jesus, and his apostles patterns (page 72) on colored cardstock paper for each child, scissors, glue or tape, and crayons

ACTIVITY: Create a Last Supper shadow box and review what happened at the Last Supper. This will help the children remember Jesus and the first sacrament. Jesus asked the apostles to take the sacrament to remember him. Each week in sacrament meeting, we take the sacrament to show Heavenly Father that we remember Jesus.
1. Color and cut out shadow box and figures.
2. Fold figure tabs.
3. Glue figure tabs in place on box.

THOUGHT TREAT: Unleavened Bread. Share with children some flat (pita) bread or fry bread, the type of bread Jesus may have served during the first sacrament (yeast free). Break some off and let the children taste it and think of the first sacrament.

I want to be a member of The Church of Jesus Christ of Latter-day Saints because I can.

*Primary 3-CTR B manual is published by The Church of Jesus Christ of Latter-day Saints, Salt Lake City, Utah.

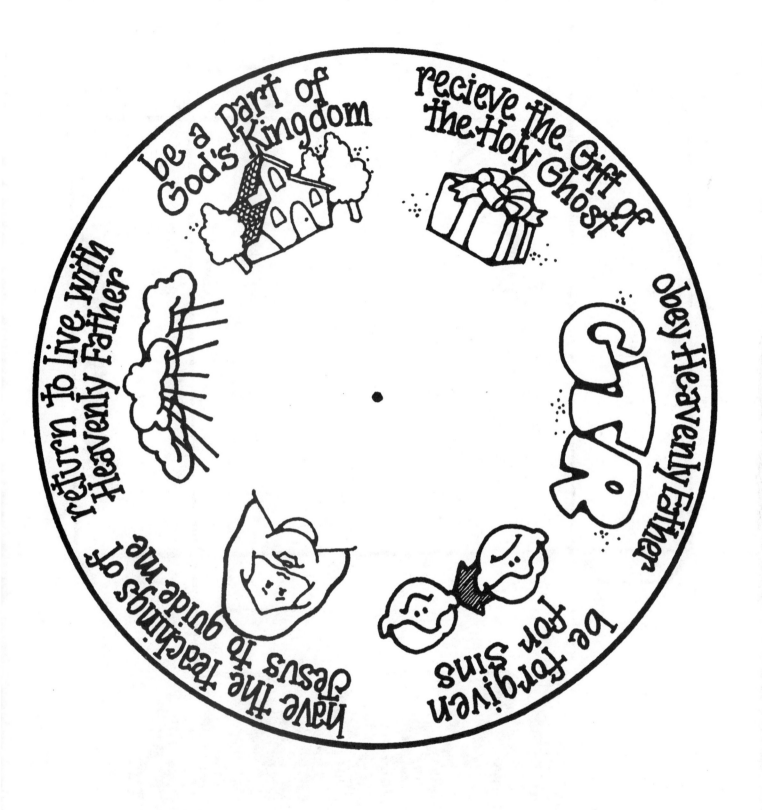

I will remember Jesus.

The Last Supper

The Sacrament

S

SACRAMENT: Reminds Us of Our Promises

(sacrament and baptism covenant flip-card)   See lesson #33 in Primary 3-CTR B manual*.

YOU'LL NEED: Copy of two-sided covenant flip-card and glue-on sticker patterns (page 74) on colored cardstock paper, and a wooden craft stick for each child, scissors, glue, and crayons

ACTIVITY: Create a two-sided flip-card to show on one side: "As I take the sacrament I will remember my baptism promises." On the other side: "I promise to: Always remember Jesus, and obey the commandments."
1. Color and cut out flip card and glue-on stickers.
2. Fold card in half.
3. Place a wooden craft stick in the center of card and glue the top half of the stick on card half way up.
4. Glue card back-to-back.
5. Glue baptism and sacrament stickers in place.

THOUGHT TREAT: Smile Face Sandwich. Make a tuna or lunch meat sandwich and place a piece of cheese with a smile face on top. Wrap sandwich or place in a plastic bag. How to Make Smile Face Cheese: Cut a square piece of cheese with a round cookie cutter or jar lid. Carve out diamond shaped eyes and nose, and round mouth. NOTE: Tell children that being baptized and taking the sacrament makes you happy because you are choosing the right, and doing what Jesus did.

SERVICE: I Serve Jesus As I Serve Others

(service with a smile badge)   See lesson #37 in Primary 3-CTR B manual*.

YOU'LL NEED: Copy of badge and smile face pattern (page 75) on colored cardstock paper, metal or button brad, and safety pin for each child, scissors, glue, and crayons

ACTIVITY: Create a service badge with a smile to show children they can show love for Jesus by helping others.
1. Color and cut out badge and smile face.
2. Poke a hole in badge where indicated and on nose, and insert metal or button brad. To Make Button Brad: Sew two buttons together on opposite sides (threading thread through the same hole) to attach smile face to badge.
3. Encourage child to turn the wheel (smile) upside down when they are not serving or helping others. When they serve or help someone, they turn the smile right side up, showing that a smile comes when you serve others. Have children say together, "I'm happy when I serve."

THOUGHT TREAT: Smile Face Crackers. Squirt processed cheese from tube or can on crackers to create smile faces. Watch the children smile as they eat.

I promise to:
- Always remember Jesus, and
- Obey the commandments.

Paste baptism picture here

As I take the sacrament I will remember my baptism promises.

Paste sacrament picture here

BAPTISM

SACRAMENT

*Primary 3-CTR B manual is published by The Church of Jesus Christ of Latter-day Saints, Salt Lake City, Utah.

T

TEMPLES & FAMILIES: Let's Be Together Forever

(temple eternity wheel)

See lesson #35 in Primary 3-CTR B manual*.

YOU'LL NEED: Copy of temple eternity wheel patterns part A and B (pages 77-78) on colored cardstock paper for each child, scissors, glue, and crayons

ACTIVITY: Create a temple eternity wheel to show children how "Families Can Be Together Forever." Wheel shows things we can do to be together forever: (1) Pay tithing, (2) Attend church, (3) Be honest, (4) Obey the Word of Wisdom, (5) Obey the commandments, and (6) Be married in the temple for eternity.
1. Color and cut out temple eternity wheel parts A and B.
2. Punch a hole in the center of parts A and B and place a metal brad in center to attach parts A and B.
3. Turn wheel to show ways families can be together forever.

THOUGHT TREAT: Temple Mints or candy mint (telling children they were "mint" to be together as a family forever)

TITHING: I Want to Pay My Tithing

(tithing bills match game)

See lesson #42 in Primary 3-CTR B manual*.

YOU'LL NEED: Copy two sets of five tithing bills patterns (page 79) on colored cardstock paper for each child, scissors, and crayons

ACTIVITY: Create a tithing match to help child know that: (1) Tithing helps build temples and meeting houses, (2) Tithing helps missionary work, (3) Tithing helps support family history and temple work, (4) Heavenly Father will bless us when we pay our tithing, and (5) I am happy to help by paying my tithing.

TO MAKE: Color and cut out tithing bills. For a larger class make two sets.
TO PLAY:
1. Mix up and turn cards face down.
2. Take turns turning two cards over for others to see.
3. If a match is made, player collects the two matching cards. Player reads the card aloud to others, i.e. "Tithing helps missionary work."
4. Play until all cards are matched and read aloud.

THOUGHT TREAT: 10 Coin Cookies. Roll out sugar cookie dough and cut into quarter-size round shapes (use a cap from a 2-liter bottle to cut cookies). Paint with cookie paints. Bake about 6-8 minutes at 350°. To Make Cookie Paints: Mix two teaspoons canned milk with food coloring. Serve 10 to children, telling them to eat 9 and give one to the bishop.

*Primary 3-CTR B manual is published by The Church of Jesus Christ of Latter-day Saints, Salt Lake City, Utah.

*Primary 3-CTR B manual is published by The Church of Jesus Christ of Latter-day Saints, Salt Lake City, Utah.

*Primary 3-CTR B manual is published by The Church of Jesus Christ of Latter-day Saints, Salt Lake City, Utah.

Tithing helps... build temples and meeting houses.

Tithing helps... missionary work.

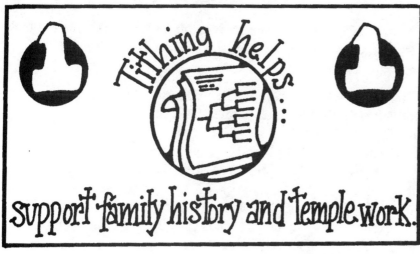

Tithing helps... support family history and temple work.

help by paying my tithing. I am happy to...

bless us when we pay tithing. Heavenly Father will...

*Primary 3-CTR B manual is published by The Church of Jesus Christ of Latter-day Saints, Salt Lake City, Utah.

79

W

WORD OF WISDOM: I Am Blessed When I Eat Healthy

(Word of Wisdom Choices)

See lesson #14 in Primary 3-CTR B manual*.

YOU'LL NEED: Copy of card and food picture patterns (pages 82-83) on colored cardstock paper and an 8 1/2" x 11" sheet of lightweight paper for each child, scissors, and crayons

ACTIVITY: Create a pocket card with two pockets. Pocket #1: Garbage can with pocket to place unhealthy foods, and Pocket #2: Mouth with pocket to place healthy foods. This activity will remind children that they are blessed with a healthy body when they follow the commandments given in the Word of Wisdom (Doctrine and Covenants 89).
1. Color and cut out card and food and substance pictures. mouth.
2. Cut slit in garbage can and mouth.
3. Create a pocket by gluing sides and bottom of the back 1/4" to an 8 1/2" x 11" sheet of paper leaving top open to hold food.

THOUGHT TREAT: Healthy Foods. Share a variety of good smelling, great tasting, tempting good-for-you foods, i.e.: Apple, celery with peanut butter, turkey, pretzels, dried fruit, or bananas.

WORSHIPPING AT CHURCH: I Want to Worship at Church

(Sunday block game)

See lesson #40 in Primary 3-CTR B manual*.

YOU'LL NEED: Copy of "I Want to Worship at Church" Sunday block game pattern (page 84) on colored cardstock paper for each child, scissors, glue, and crayons

ACTIVITY: Show ways to enjoy worshipping at church.
1. Color and cut out Sunday block game.
2. Fold game into a block.
3. Fold flaps inside block and glue.
TO PLAY THE SUNDAY BLOCK GAME:
1. Take turns rolling one block.
2. Each side of the die (block) shows a way that we can worship at church. For example, if "sacrament" lands face up, have the child tell how we can worship during the sacrament. For "listen," have child tell what we can learn as we listen. For "sing," have child give his favorite Primary song. For "pray," have child say what we can pray for.
3. When block lands on the girl and boy, ask a girl or boy in class what they like about coming to church on Sunday.
4. When block lands on "I Want to Worship at Church" say, "I want to worship at church."

THOUGHT TREAT: Hard Tack Candy. As children suck on candy they can think of how quiet we must be while we worship at church.

*Primary 3-CTR B manual is published by The Church of Jesus Christ of Latter-day Saints, Salt Lake City, Utah.

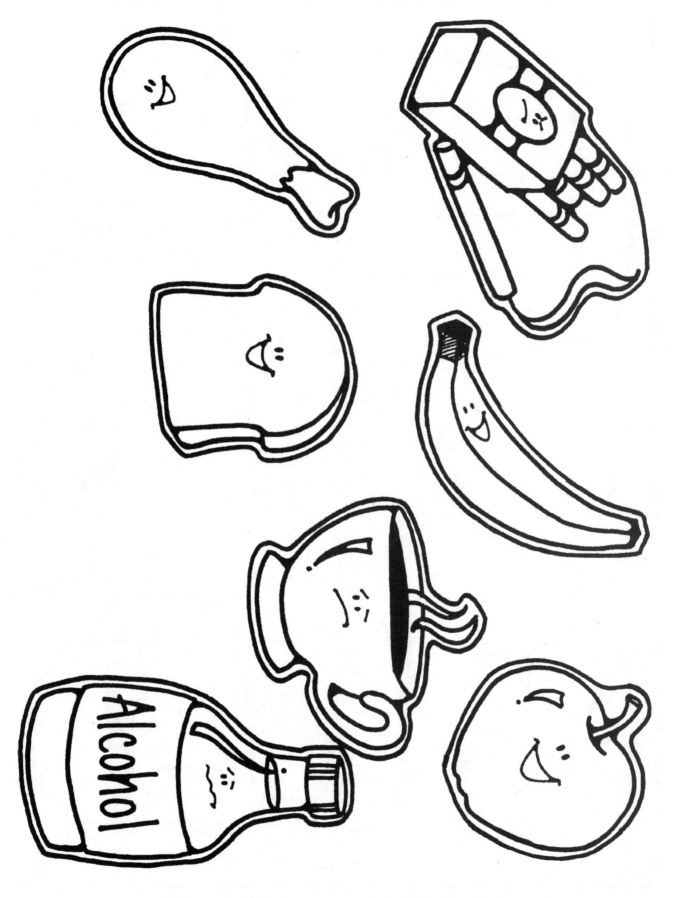

Dear Parents:
This is

_____'s

**I Can Bear
My Testimony
CTR Fun Box.**

Each week,
please encourage
your child to display
the activity creations
made in Primary or
family home evening.
Your child's
testimony can grow
by showing you the
visuals and telling
you about lessons
learned.
Store these
testimony treasures in
this, their very own
CTR Fun Box.

Thank you.

_____
Primary Teacher

GLUE TO BOX LID

Glue to box bottom Left side

Glue to box bottom Right side

Glue to box back Right side

Glue to box back Left side

I CAN BEAR MY TESTIMONY CTR FUN BOX

More *PRIMARY PARTNERS*

Each activity is listed alphabetically and cross-referenced to a particular lesson in the Primary manuals. With appealing art work and fun-to-do games and crafts children will remember the message taught. Use these every week in Primary, of course ... but don't forget family home evening, where the good times get even better.

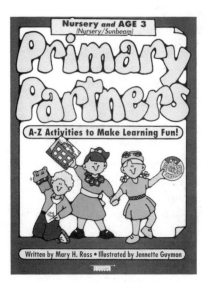

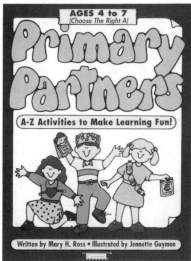

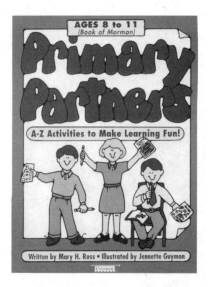

With this Nursery and Age 3 volume you can help a toddler appreciate the scriptures, and understand what it means to be reverent. You'll enjoy the 46 fun and unique crafts and activities contained in this book. Even the youngest children can learn important gospel principles.

For example, this temple tie and tithing purse is send home as a reminder that families can be forever.

Some Activities Are:
♥ Example sandals to follow Jesus
♥ I Have "Bean" Obedient bean bag
♥ Bird watch and bug jar
♥ Family face block
♥ Reverent mouse maze
♥ Family prayer fan
♥ Fish Bowl, fish and pole
♥ Smile and frown flip-flag
♥ Animals Help Me sticker fun
♥ 3-D Noah's ark

To help children ages 4-7 Choose The Right, enjoy using this Primary 2-CTR A volume to send them home with fun visuals: A pair of resurrection glasses to make the statement, "All eyes can see again!" Or, they can wear a band-aid bandelo to show that "When it is sick that I am feeling, I'll let the priesthood do the healing." These growing spirits can learn about tithing, service, forgiveness, reverence and ... MORE:
♥ Heavenly Family Photo
♥ Choices situation slap game
♥ Ammon "script"ure scene
♥ Forgiving Faces
♥ CTR happiness wheel (above)
♥ Prayer rock poem
♥ Dare to Be True wristbands
♥ Gratitude Gopher grab bag
♥ I Love You pop-up card
♥ Scripture scroll
♥ Wise and foolish man flip-flag

As the Primary lesson subjects for ages 8-11 coordinate with the adult scriptures taught, both child and parent can enjoy reading the scriptures together year-after-year. For example, this *Primary Partners* activities match with the Book of Mormon lessons in the Primary 4 manual.

Children this age enjoy challenges to help them develop faith in Jesus Christ, put on the armor of God, keep baptismal covenants, and be a good example, like the heroes found in the Book of Mormon.

Some Testimony Builders Are:
♥ Fight for Right! word choice
♥ 3-D box with Tree of Life Vision
♥ Nephite & Lamanite peace poster
♥ Waters of Mormon word search

Mary H. Ross, Author and
Jennette Guymon, Illustrator
are also the creators of:

SUPER SCRIPTURE ACTIVITIES:
▫ New Testament--I'm Trying to Be Like Jesus
▫ New Testament--Tell Me the Stories of Jesus
▫ New Testament--Jesus Is My Friend

PRIMARY PARTNERS:
A-Z Activities to Make Learning Fun for:
▫ Nursery and Age 3 (Sunbeams)
▫ CTR A & B Ages 4-7
▫ Book of Mormon Ages 8-11 (and more)
▫ Achievement Days Ages 8-11

MARY H. ROSS, Author

Mary Ross is an energetic mother, Primary teacher, and Achievement Days leader for two years, who loves to help children have a good time while they learn. She is a published author and columnist who has studied acting and taught modeling and voice. Her varied interests include writing, creating activities and children's parties, and cooking. Mary and her husband, Paul, live with their daughter, Jennifer in Sandy, Utah.

- Photos by Scott Hancock, Provo, Utah

JENNETTE GUYMON, Illustrator

Jennette Guymon has studied graphic arts and illustration at Utah Valley State College and the University of Utah. She is currently employed with a commercial construction company. She served a mission to Japan. Jennette enjoys sports, reading, cooking, art, and freelance illustrating. Jennette lives in Riverton, Utah.

ENJOY SUPER SCRIPTURE ACTIVITIES:

♥ In these activity books, you will find creative ways to help children become familiar with the scriptures and have fun, too! ♥ These 12 *Super Scripture Activities* tell exciting New Testament stories, relate the scriptures to everyday life, and involve children in lively, memorable activities that will keep them interested and entertained (not to mention learning!) for hours at a time.

♥ Whether you like things simple or more elaborate, these activities are for you! It's your choice--do a little or a lot with these amazingly versatile plans and ideas. Use them for Primary sharing time, family home evening, classroom activities, 2 1/2 minute talks, or even a friendly neighborhood get-together. You'll all be in for a great time!

THEMES:
Heavenly Treasures
Seeds of Faith
In His Steps
Trying to Be Like Jesus
Choosing The Right
Celebrating Birth of Jesus
Angel Tells of Two Births
Fishers of Men
The Gifts He Gave
Blessed Beatitudes
Service with a Smile
Jesus Is Our Life Savior

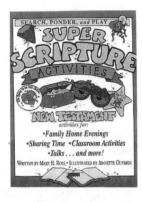